ARCHITECTURE FOR CARS

CHRISTOPHER BEANLAND

ARCHITECTURE FOR CARS

CHRISTOPHER BEANLAND

HOW CARS
SHAPED MODERN
ARCHITECTURE

BATSFORD

CONTENTS

Flyover in Hong Kong,
China

INTRODUCTION

It's the rhythm of the road that gets me. The syncopation of tyres travelling over tarmac with the thrum of an engine, the beat of music in the background, mixed with all the other vehicles, with chatter, with gusting winds. If all of history up to this point was largely about staying in place, the modern age was truly about speed and movement, about distance and the psychological feel of traversing that flattened landscape.

In my previous book, *Station*, I wrote about how railways had sped up the world, stretched the possible, linked people and places, altered our worlds and the worlds in our heads. Cars would change the game again because we weren't the passenger — we were the driver.

The turning wheels revolve endlessly and go nowhere as the vehicle moves forward with us in it. The orbit echoes that of the planet the fiendish machine is going to destroy. The wheel we grip is circular. Everything moves forwards but it also doesn't. It tricks us into thinking that. We're not going forwards at all — we're glued by gravity to this planet, we're revolving on an axis and we're spinning round the sun, and our lives go in a big circle from a helpless birth to a helpless death. We cast out in the middle like a swingball to enjoy the best of our lives when we are in control of them before returning to the bat, to the family and the drudgery and the predictable path.

But what a life we can make it in the middle. And the chance to now be able to explore Earth's great limits is a wish from the genie. We rubbed the lamp. To pull in for a breakfast burrito in sight of Monument Valley, to traverse the pock-marked ash of Hawaii's Big Island, to cross a whole continent (and stop for golf on the Nullarbor), to be able to creep close to Volcan de Agua and see it spitting fire across a Guatemalan sky — kids dream of adventure and now we have that chance. Nothing is stopping us from grabbing those opportunities.

Driving gives us the illusion of power and freedom. All these things are possible. They seem possible. All avenues are open. Car advertising sells us this dream. But driving atomizes us. It remakes us into grumpy, speed-obsessed individuals competing with others — the perfect capitalist citizens in other words.

I'm telling you right now, as I've done before, to quit your pointless jobs and make every second count as if it's your last. But all you do is use the car as a runabout. Most cars trundle to Tesco and back, take the kids to the in-laws up the

Previous page: East Cross Route / A12, London, UK

This page: Flyover in Peshawar, Pakistan

motorway and ferry one of the family to a job that will probably have been automated in the time between me writing these words and this book hitting the shelves. You don't even really know if it's me, Christopher Beanland, writing right now or an AI? Even more reason to take a punt on what really matters — but make sure it's done compassionately and offset your carbon, thanks.

Ballard said the defining image of the 20th century was the person in the car. Those times have passed now. Although cars can give us adventure we must be mindful too — get on your bike, walk — why the hell do you have a car in the city? But for some great adventures, well, the car and the motel and the drive-thru are the guilty pleasures of the age. As with smoking and drinking and eating meat, driving will seem so passé to the youngsters of the next century, if we make it that far. Cars will rebrand and run on turnips. But we'll still need to move. Yes, we must protect the Earth, and yes, we have to change; we have to basically stop all consumption. But we still need to move, to explore, to meet, to see, to hear, to taste, to love, to learn — these things are too important to say we're just going to sit at home forever.

The open road was sold as a dream. Maybe you think I've been suckered. It's worth pointing out not a penny from car or oil companies has been syphoned into my bank account to write

this book — though one previous potential publisher suggested we should get it sponsored by one of them. Hmm. When those oil and car companies see what I'm about to say about them, they'll be glad they didn't put up any cash. Yet, I'm as taken in as anyone by the dream — particularly by the American dream — of an individual and abundant world driven by technology. And one where the National Parks were reachable and you could fuel up on burgers on the way there. Yes, it stinks. But to a younger me it was catnip. Maybe it still is.

ROADS

As Jonathan Meades pointed out, the Fens of England have a kindred spirit — not just in the Netherlands as you'd expect but in the American country-and-western belt. It's ironic that growing up here the thing I wanted the most was America — its music, its films, its sneakers; I wanted to be there. Yet the thing I hated the most was long drives, and these are at the heart of any American adventure. Maybe it was the 'being driven'. And it wasn't the long drives so much as the shit roads. The A17 drove me bananas; how I envied those who lived off the A1 and could get everywhere so quickly.

I mention all this not out of narcissism or laziness but because the experience of driving and roads is a very personal one. We could say the experience of life itself is too, now that society is so grossly atomized and capitalism has delivered individuality par excellence. I could talk about the great movements and the history of roads and the structures near them (and I will) but it's a peculiarly personal thing too. You will already be thinking, I'm sure, about your own childhood, about the routes you took to see family and to go on holiday, to go on day trips or to the supermarket. The things you saw, the places you stopped, the food you ate.

THE BEGINNINGS

The revolution began quaintly with *The Wind in The Willows* and with Lord De La Warr racing cars along Bexhill seafront on what would later become the site of one of England's greatest buildings, the streamline moderne De La Warr Pavillion, and *Chitty Chitty Bang Bang* eccentricity. These were playthings for the rich but the democratization of the means would in time cause enormous changes.

London's green cab shelters come from the age when horses pulled vehicles – we still talk about how much horsepower cars have. Slowly, life adapted with the first one-way systems and houses with garages in Birmingham. Road houses – pubs on a huge scale but with heightened ambitions – landed by arterial roads in Stirchley and Northfield in Birmingham too.

Cars and lorries needed fuel. Arne Jacobsen's petrol station and the British modernist petrol stations were where you filled up. Even more outré gas-station designs emerged in the Eastern bloc, where Ladas needed to move somehow. Oil was going to be the must-have commodity – BP took a keen interest in Persia. Standard Oil was becoming an imperial-like player. Geopolitics shifted dramatically. Nodding donkeys became American icons. Wars were for black gold. Are they still? Unfortunately, yes.

FREEWAYS OF LIVING

The Futurama exhibition at the 1939 New York World's Fair is a key moment in the story. The expo was a kind of internet of its day – where you could indulge in visions and ideas brought to life in a more immediate way than by just leafing through a book. Here Norman Bel Geddes' ambitious model of a 1960s future America was brought to lavish life, and visitors rode round seeing with their own eyes what awaited them. It was completely prescient. Other pavilions at expos by General Motors, Ford and Shell promoted similar visions.

But could we not have had this and also kept the railway lines that connected and transformed 19th-century America (and so many other countries)? Imagine a world with the transport best of both.

TVAM building /
former garage,
Camden, UK

Germany built its first autobahns during a disgraceful period of forced labour and concentration camps. The Four Level Interchange in LA opened and the first parkways threaded up the Arroyo Seco Valley to Pasadena and the Hudson Valley in New York.

The civil engineering ingenuity involved in building these projects should not be underestimated. Chris Marshall is Britain's road expert and reminds us about the M62:

Scammonden Dam on the M62, and the bridge crossing the motorway just next to it. The motorway passes through a man-made cutting, which is not unusual, but the scale of this particular one is in a league of its own. The material excavated from the cutting was used to build a dam, big enough to carry the motorway on top, which holds back a reservoir a mile in length that swallowed a whole village. The cutting is so wide and so deep that, when it was built, the bridge spanning it was the longest single-span non-suspension bridge in the world. The bridge is simply there to carry a B road. It's a motorway built with enormous effort and ingenuity across more unforgiving terrain than any other road in the UK, and as a feat of civil engineering it deserves far more recognition than it ever gets.

SPEED

With trains the world speeded up, with cars it speeded up more. Now we were passing through space at a more and more frantic rate. Eventually speed limits were the end result. The fact that the built environment, like the countryside, flew past at a rate of knots changed our perception of buildings. Architects responded with kitsch flourishes to grab a driver's attention.

The elastic change in time the car brought about meant that we could commute. We could live further and further from our jobs — not in the next shabby street next to a factory. Cities could then be zoned with housing away from industry, commerce and retail. And new cities could emerge, their neighbourhoods connected by highways.

It was inevitable of course that once fast cars appeared people would try and race them. The boy racers on country lanes became the bored lads speeding along Belle Isle Road or around Chelmsley Wood and Nechells Parkway.

When this was formalized it was obvious that motor sport's drama was going to be a big draw. The AVUS circuit in Berlin, Goodwood, Monza — the motor-racing circuits became huge entities, and Formula 1 in particular has kept reinventing itself to become a global phenomenon. Monaco's street race is the cordon bleu — the

strange experience of being there, though, is glimpsing just a flicker of something between the fences, not really sensing the track entirely. Even at a conventional circuit the experience is intense and jarring — the extreme noise and not knowing who is where. Birmingham famously tried to recreate this as the 'Monaco of the Midlands' in the late 80s — turning over their ring road and streets to the racing cars.

Unsurprisingly, TV lapped up this hobby. Murray Walker's voice commentating on Prost versus Senna is a memory that will never leave me. The newer circuits have been designed as beacons of modernity really — the Formula 1 brand of luxury, drama, speed, skill, precision — these are what Jeddah, Bahrain, Singapore, Kuala Lumpur, Austin, Baku, Abu Dhabi, have wanted to be aligned with. The legendary circuits like Le Mans (home of the 24 Hour race) and Spa have deep histories.

Those who like to speed know that German autobahns almost alone have no limits. Elsewhere the speed camera, or 'radar' as it's known in many European languages, has kept us in check — that yellow or grey camera on a pole or mounted above the road, a symbol like the CCTV camera and intelligent display of a tech-oriented road of the future. Purists eschew this surveillance and enjoy the German road with its noticeable lack of clutter and tech.

Sainsbury's, Camden, UK

BUSES

The car was glamorous. At least it was supposed to be. The bus? Not quite so much. But it's cheap (sometimes), cheerful and gets the job done. All kids get the bus – to school and on school trips. You learn about exploring and bravery from bus journeys, not from being driven round in mollycoddling mums' SUVs. The school trip is always by bus. When the railways and streetcars/trams were on their way out, they were replaced by buses.

The feeling was the bus could be a more efficient form of transport than trams and trains – the bus could go everywhere the tracks could not. Uh-oh. That went well – because buses, alas, are not as good as trains. They're still great, but trains are better, trams too. Look at the dozens and dozens of cities trying to bring back tramways removed in the haste of the car-crazy decades.

This streetcar conspiracy was ridiculous and, yes, we have learned many times it was of course perpetuated by our old friends the auto, oil and tyre lobbies. Some architectural gifts were given among the scandalous wastage. Busáras in Dublin; Derby and Preston's bus stations. Tel Aviv's is too much but cannot be missed. The Port Authority Bus Terminal? Well, it's hair-raising, but then so much about life in New York is. Victoria Coach Station in London came with art deco glamour when it opened.

The Eastern bloc bus shelter became a cult with its own books. Canberra's cute bus shelters became an icon of the new city. The bus lane became a symbol of segregation on the road – an attempt to make the experience of sitting on the rickety bus a little less annoying. The guided busway or bus rapid transport tried to elevate the bus to almost the level of the tram. Adelaide's O-Bahn sails through a river valley on a concrete track that made me think of a Disneyland experimental transport system when I saw it.

Latterly the bus has made a comeback. Skopje bought bright-red double-deckers like London. Manchester has taken its buses back into civic hands and painted them all yellow.

Of course, some people didn't used to even buy a bus ticket, and hitchhiking – its hopeful participants gathering on the roundabouts and junctions at the edge of towns eager for a free ride – has come and gone in the UK. In many countries hitchhiking is still a run-of-the-mill way of getting around. Apps like BlaBlaCar have even projected a kind of 21st-century hitching into our data-driven worlds.

WHAT WE SAW

The signs that point us towards places lose their importance as times move on and we are guided ever more seamlessly by computers. Signposts, tag-teamed with maps, used to be the only way

Port Authority Bus Terminal, New York City

to know where to go. Reading a map was an essential skill. Everyone had an A–Z street atlas. The general road atlas sold by the bucketload and one sat on every passenger seat when the route calculations were something you did yourself by looking at the roads towards your destination. Thinking in 2D and 3D were great skills. Driving involves numerous calculations and that's why it is a process that can probably be fully automated. But those maps were also things of beauty in their own right. The shapes of the cities and the lines the roads followed across the country were fascinating to behold.

THE COUNTRYSIDE

Rural locations lost their rail connections, while some places are so remote or so underpopulated they never even had that. Cars were the new horses. It seems barmy that our tarmac arteries connect almost everywhere — largely funded by the state. Growing up in the countryside, rural roads were the connective tissue between places and people. The things you see — the old signposts, the wiggly lanes, the sunken roads bearing witness to hundreds of years of travels, the coaching inns, the blind summits and dangerous junctions — are testament to a world remade for the driver. Every house now with a garage and a car in the drive, whether in the real country or the suburbs that pretended to be the country and which architectural critic Ian Nairn railed at in the 1950s.

The rural petrol station with one pump, the passing place, the drunk drivers (no taxis), the tractors, the harvest, the hedgerows. And the main roads that pass through the rural idyll, bringing the metropolis with them: the noise, the lights, the signs, the bridges and underpasses. From the main road slicing through the pastures you can spy a countryside that seems like a theme park but is far more serious. And the main road brings its own architecture to the countryside: the service station, the picnic spot, the strip mall and the retail outlets at junctions, out-of-town office parks and supermarkets.

Bypasses bring the road into the fields — the village or the town gets its streetlife back but the people living on the peripheries now have cars at the end of their gardens. (One of the weirdest bypasses ever built is the Cinta Costera viaduct, which loops round Panama City's old town out over the ocean on stilts.)

CITIES

Whereas the car makes a sort of sense in the country and other options are limited, the city was always going to be a bigger problem. You see the traffic jams in cities with incredible public transport like Brussels, New York, Munich and Paris and wonder why there's even a car there at all. Trains, trams, buses, bikes, walking: the country doesn't have these options, but the city does. How did we get here?

The planners thought the car would simply be everywhere and that everyone would have one. You watch the documentaries from the 60s that talk about cities having their arteries clogged but their solution is not give up the fags, booze and burgers — it's install more arteries so you can do all those things even more.

The planners assumed that we would simply have to rebuild the city for the car. And if that didn't work we would build new cities like Brasilia and Cumbernauld and Chorweiler and Louvain-la-Neuve and Milton Keynes and the deadening sprawl of Halle-Neustadt (aka Ha-Neu for the jokers) that were specifically designed for drivers, even though the East German citizens had to patiently wait for their awful Trabbie.

The city was changed beyond all recognition. The carchitecture age ('carchitecture' being shorthand for the car-centric architecture we saw emerge in the 20th Century and even more rapidly in the post-WWII world) brought in the one-way system, the gyratory, the urban motorway, the traffic light. Then it was the speed camera, the number plate recognition camera, the *Black Mirror* monitoring of the whole system. Roads cut communities as well as linking others. The Joy Division bridge in Manchester, where the band were famously photographed in the snow, bridged a chasm created by a new road, by a new world: the image and the music represented the nihilism of the new isolated age.

All those cars came into the city and needed somewhere to go. The car park was an eyesore no one wanted to live next to but it had a strange beauty too. The Hanielgarage in Düsseldorf was the work of Paul Schneider, as Felix Torkar of the SOS Brutalism project points out. Schneider gifted Germany a car park and a soundtrack to the car age: his son Florian founded Kraftwerk and made electronic elegies to the autobahn, the repeated rhythms echoing the strange posture of driving — exciting and boring all at once. Bristol and Leicester pioneered the car park. Paul Rudolph gave us New Haven's legendary structure. The Welbeck Street car park off Oxford Street in London had legions of admirers who tried to save it from demolition in later years. Leeds and Birmingham had automated garages — you still see these in Manhattan. Some car parks were buried under office blocks, shopping centres and public squares. I thought this era was over yet Vienna installed a new one under the Neuer Markt complete with vehicle access tunnels in the early 2020s — only 60 years late to that party.

Colin Buchanan's orthodoxy was followed closely around the world — the *Traffic In Towns* idea illustrated by those cutesy colour cartoons that were 'town planner porn': you wanted to separate people from traffic. Ideally with the cars below. The visions for Irvine New Town in Scotland were so slickly rendered that they constitute art — powerful blue and white graphics that ooze sci-fi glamour. With Meriadeck, the Barbican, Thamesmead, Leeds city centre, Birmingham city centre, the City of London, Cologne, you see pretty full-scale attempts to bring this vision to life. At numerous social housing projects the idea was promulgated.

If there's one glaring problem that I had to admit to with the brutalist project, it is exactly this accommodation with cars and the attempt to split levels. Because what you so often end up with is this dark, dank, subterranean world where you weren't supposed to go but somehow always ended up needing to. Humans could not always stay up on the walkways — you needed to descend to ground level to get to a car or take out the trash or meet someone who's lost. These eerie spaces below scared the shit out of good people. Likewise the subways under the road and the bridges over it were never places any of us wanted to be. Desire lines prove the point — we'd often rather take our chances. This is me to

a tee — I could not tell you the number of fences and central reservations I have vaulted to get somewhere quicker. Yet I'm probably unusual in being drawn like a moth to the flame when it comes to those frightening undercrofts too. They are the places where monsters and melodrama hide; in my novel *The Wall in the Head* I give the main character the opportunity to circulate in this world under Birmingham and he can't stop himself. He finds himself dragged into this Ballardian netherworld beneath Masshouse and Paradise Circus, where the noise and the smell and the smoke and the homeless mix. The realities did not match the visions. It is horrible but horribly compelling, like an immersive horror film. But these spaces can be inhabited for good, by skaters or by Coventry's poets and artists who create beneath its ring road.

Even on a more quotidian level the car recreated the city. Benches, bins, bollards, streetlights, parking meters, advertising boards, fences, drains, manhole covers: the things we never notice. Traffic lights — I love how they're called 'robots' in South Africa — maintained a flow. Traffic towers like the 1924 one in Potsdamer Platz or the leaning ones across the Eastern Bloc perched over junctions. In Bermuda's capital, Hamilton, the policeman on a plinth directing traffic is a famous sight. Pavements or sidewalks are there to stop

Potsdamer Platz, Berlin

pedestrians sleepwalking into traffic. Crossings are needed to get across roads. Different surfaces keep people away from roads, railings block places where lazy walkers might cut across a dual carriageway. We are being managed. We are all being managed though – drivers, cyclists, walkers.

You can't see the modernist project without the road and the car. After all, this is what the architects and planners of the time thought and were told was the transport of that age. Rockefeller Plaza in Albany came with underground parking, Paradise Circus and the Bull Ring in Birmingham both came with underground bus stations. Canberra was laid out once for the car with wide roads everywhere, then again in the brutalist era when the city centre was to be jacked up a storey, with our old friend the podium placing everything a layer above the traffic like a sandwich – as the National Gallery of Australia now somewhat weirdly demonstrates in the context of a half-executed plan. Transport was baked in – intimately at an urban level or always with a ground-floor car park next to a building if not. The Westin Bonaventure sits astride Downtown LA next to off-ramps and with its own walkways and parking lots, its cylinders somehow trying to rise above the melee in the way that its twin, the even taller Renaissance Center, does in Detroit.

One a hotel for drivers, the other the HQ of a car company – General Motors. As with malls, they strip cars out of the generous atria. But on the outside it's less calm and more chaos.

I sometimes wonder how different the project would have been if the architects were not in thrall to the internal combustion engine. If there weren't such rabbit warrens and level shifts, might Portsmouth's Tricorn and Birmingham Central Library have been spared the wrecking ball? Welbeck Street car park had a culty second life with a branch of MEATliquor slinging burgers in 2012 in the basement and hipsters queuing up round the block to wait for a table. Fluc in Vienna turned a subway under a roundabout into a cool music venue. It's strange how things change.

It was really the levels that did for a lot of these buildings. If you wanted to grade-separate a road junction, you ended up with these spaghetti subways. No one builds like this now (except the A100 extension in Berlin, a perplexing outlier) – boulevards with surface crossings, trees and cycle lanes have become the norm instead, but the over-engineered motorway still has the shock-and-awe power when you see it, when you are swallowed by it.

BUYING

Cars were an intensely capitalist outcome. Every time anyone talks about individual freedom they mean the freedom to spend in ever more creative ways. A means of transport you had to buy and you had to buy the fuel for? What a racket. Also something where you could immediately see the owner's position within the class structure. Don't forget the many who couldn't even get on the car ladder. Or look at the scooter riders in Asia piling up the cargo on the back.

Yes, purchasing was always inherent in the model. Why not get the new drivers to drive to the shops and buy more crap? The motor age was perfectly suited to getting people to buy more than they could carry. Supermarkets were the obvious corollary. The entire world is now dotted with roadside superstores. Some looked brilliant, like the brutalist GEM store in France, some bonkers like the Tesco inside Leicester's first multi-storey car park. The hypermarket took it even further – enormous Walmarts selling guns, boats and BBQs; I am rather partial to their T-shirts though – is that bad? The British 'farm barn' style of supermarkets from the 1980s is as hilarious as you'd expect from a country that just does not see how utterly weird it is.

Malls were the next ruse. City-centre redevelopment brought multi-storey shopping centres complete with parking, and transformed towns, while on the periphery of cities the mega-malls landed. Clean, strange worlds emerged inside the halls of the mall. Sterilized fun with a background of logos, conversation pits and fountains. The film *Mallrats* picks it all apart, as does Catherine O'Flynn's bravura novel *What Was Lost*. The latter peeps behind the curtain to show the passageways and backdoors that bring the retail theatre to life.

Cars themselves needed to be bought – then fixed when they inevitably went wrong. Showrooms and garages emerged on every high street and latterly in every industrial estate on the edge of town. Rootes in Maidstone is a moderne gem as celebrated by Historic England in its Grade II listing. It's a Howard and Souster work from 1939 with slinky white lines like a lido. The HQ and depot of Michelin in Chelsea became a restaurant and so the link between tyres and dining was cemented – Michelin's guides to eating were originally a marketing tie-in to flog tyres and tell drivers where they could stop for a good bite. The brutalist Mercedes dealership in Coruña with its famous 'Merc in the sky' has become a stalwart of Insta #brutalist feeds even after its demolition. The K Garage, now a Nissan showroom, sits right by the M1 near its London terminus. You are designed to pass the raw concrete box at speed. Slow down and you see the details like the glazed ramps and clocks. It is an icon of that age.

I was too young for these of course – my car showroom memories are of the cookie-cutter

Border post, Georgia

shops, each scrupulously clean, ostentatiously so, and at odds with the muck and reality of a 'garage' where work takes place, where oil is changed and filthy overalls and mugs of tea and jacks are the order of business. These showrooms create a fantasy world where cars don't pollute and their insides are not full of sweet wrappers and dander. The 'new car smell' prevails. There were toy cars and brochures, and full-size cars you could sit in, and the salespeople appeared polite. These stores could be rolled out internationally; each car brand's variety was slightly different. As a kid you would learn the mass-market brand logos so the words almost didn't matter — Peugeot, Renault, Citroen, Ford, Vauxhall, Seat, Skoda, VW.

Your dad's company car was his obsession — a direct and obvious show of where he was in the pecking order. Promotion equalled the journey from Fiesta to Escort to Sierra to Granada. Ballard drove the latter, and I never really worked out why. It seemed like the car he drove — just like the house he picked on a quiet road in Shepperton — was a kind of satirical gesture against the status quo. Of course he walked round the garden in the nude. As a kid with an eye for cars (thanks, Dad) even I could see the Ford Granada was like a whale. The Cortina was more me.

CONNECTIONS

Roads and cars meant bridges and tunnels. 'Bridge and Tunnel' is an often pejorative term used to describe someone who isn't from Manhattan, who drives in. Now with these roads above and below, rivers and even seas were no longer barriers.

The UFO Bridge in Bratislava made its modernist point. When we humans see a massive river or a gorge between us and where we want to get to, it's human instinct to want to build a socking great bridge over the gap. Despite what politicians might make some of us think we want, the one urge we truly have is to be connected to everyone else. Bridges are the symbolic glue that binds us together.

Today's superbridges are being built longer and higher than ever — the Jiaozhou Bay Bridge in China is 26km (16 miles) long, while Lord Foster's Millau Viaduct in France is taller than the Eiffel Tower. We seem to have a new appetite for show-off bridges too.

These are austere times. We can't afford to dream quite like our forebears did, yet some dreams are hard to shake off — plans for ever longer and more elaborate bridges just seem to keep coming back, like a villain who refuses to die at the end of a slasher movie. Superbridges linking Italy to Sicily, Malta to Gozo, Spain to Morocco, Argentina to Uruguay, Russia to Alaska, and even Britain to Ireland, have all been on the drawing board.

Borders still separate us. Some of the modernist crossing points that dotted Europe just stand as reminders of how dumb borders can be and how time-wasting it is to cross them. Some of them are very attractive though. Although borders should never be encouraged, J.Mayer.H's Georgian border crossings are at least imposing and quirky sights by the roadside.

We've heard a lot about cars, but lorries were an integral part of this moment too. The destruction of the railways left them to run riot. Did we foresee the end point of that game would be Daventry International Rail Freight Terminal and the like? These distribution parks on a head-scratching scale whose architecture is that of the XXXL shed; white, sometimes with coloured stripes and a corporate logo — a giant sea of nothingness more alienating even than the motorways which sliced through the towns. The new ecology of Europe and the US is these nodes along the motorways in the middle of the country from where your shoelaces are delivered the next day or your lettuce gets to Sainsbury's in the middle of the night. Across the world the distribution depot seamlessly maintains the capitalist status quo — providing us with everything we desire as we cruise the online world, clicking and looking

for succour in purchasing. The decline of town centres and malls has only exacerbated this movement towards 'delivery'; the tech means it can be managed at scale — even predicted. The machines know what we want before we do.

FREEWAY REVOLTS

Was it any wonder that we would turn against roads? Even in the 1930s Pasadena voters weren't keen on the new freeway coming to town. Opposition has only grown. Numerous well-known freeway revolts sparked in San Francisco, Phoenix, Malibu, Miami, Chicago, London and Berlin.

People saw what the freeways did and they didn't like it. Especially if it was coming to tear through your neighbourhood. There was a dark dynamic — the demolition of Claiborne Avenue in New Orleans and the slash-and-burn approach of the Cross Bronx Expressway seemed particularly targeted at Black neighbourhoods. Urban planner Robert Moses was not an ally. Adam Susaneck's brilliantly shocking visualizations on @segregation_by_design show freeways ploughing through Black districts in Tulsa and Minneapolis, and it seems impossible to see anything other than a racist imperative.

In Britain anti-roads protests exploded in the 1990s — I know because when I was at university I was actively studying Swampy and

the Twyford Down protests and the M11 Link activists in Wanstead who clung to trees and roofs while the bulldozers and security guards surrounded them. Artist Graeme Miller's house was demolished for the M11 Link and after the new road opened he installed radio transmitters along it which would broadcast memories of former residents as a memento mori.

Driving seemed so fun and then when you finally saw the suffering that it could bring, it left a nasty taste in the mouth. The journalist and activist Jane Jacobs crossed over into the mainstream so much that she's even a character in *The Marvelous Mrs Maisel* — a wonderful period touch — protesting the LOMEX highway that threatened to carve thorough Lower Manhattan and which most people could see was a step too far. In the future, roads in the West would perhaps be buried or hidden. In Asia it is a different story — there's no shyness about building huge roads and infrastructure in Egypt or China or India. Indeed, China's whole foreign policy MO in the 2020s

Car showroom, M1, London

is this long-distance international road-building initiative – a 'new Silk Road' – while maximizing motorways on home turf.

Society has become totally split, the fracture encouraged at every stage by politicians, because only a solid movement can challenge them, and by business, because catering to every conceivable whim (and many that are not yet conceivable) is good for the bottom line. We are used to having everything our own way and our patience is thin. Transport has become this depressing war. We need to listen to the calm voices of reason, like Simon Calder, who extols the virtues of all types of travel – from hiking to hitch-hiking to cycling to trains to planes – because, for him and for the intelligentsia it is the journey as well as the destination that matters. Sadly we have seen division stoked at every corner – cyclist pitched against motorist, drivers against railway riders, fighting over parking at the school gate. There's nothing to be gained from squabbling among ourselves and it distracts us from shining a light at the powerful – this is exactly what they want.

I've written a book about roads and cars and I've never owned a car. I cycle everywhere in London and I can't go into town without a driver moaning at me for one thing or another. But I understand it. Getting behind the wheel isolates you. It's the ultimate capitalist act. It turns you into a different person. You feel more monstrous and after a few days you can see yourself changing in the rear-view mirror like the Incredible Hulk – this happens to me when I'm driving a rental through Utah or the Levante.

Hamburg, Seoul, Medellín, Madrid, Boston, Seattle and San Francisco have advocated removing or burying highways to free up space and make pedestrians' lives easier. Utrecht slammed a motorway into the trench where the Catharijnesingel Canal ran through the city centre in the 70s – then ripped it all out and flooded it again in the last decade – and hoped no one would notice that strange half a century of highways within the hundreds of years of history of the canal and the city.

As these eccentric and outdated environments vanish worldwide, a new generation is increasingly interested in documenting them. They'll need to be quick: in 2015, subways that threaded south through Coventry's ring road to its impressively airy Grade II-listed train station were torn out. The transformation of this part of the city continues apace.

The reimagining of carchitecture has seen flyovers turned into public parks, roadside chain restaurants become American diners, car showrooms turned into shops. The Armstrong rubber factory office in New Haven was transformed into Hilton's Hotel Marcel. Car-park roofs in Peckham, Lisbon and Berlin became Franks, Park and Kumpelnest bars. In Leeds the former petrol station on the road to Headingley has been turned into the city's coolest venue — and the one I'm always most excited to call in at on book tours. Thanks to Jack and David for always making me feel so welcome at Hyde Park Book Club — where you can catch jazz and comedy one night, and some blonde idiot wanging on about architecture the next.

Underground car parks have become art galleries and one in central London was even converted into London's first underground hotel — the Zedwell. The amount of adaptive reuse you see around the world is almost endless. It's a fascinating extra layer to a story that is not as simple as it seems, as I've tried to show. The environmentally profligate age gave us pains in the neck but also opportunities. At Birmingham's Ringway Centre, Extinction Rebellion actively campaigned to save a building and essentially a whole street which was as emblematic of the car age as it's possible to be. The answer now is not to knock it all down and start again. The carbon that's embedded in these schemes can be leveraged by reusing, getting creative, and seeing the value in what was made in these times. Berlin's Bierpinsel lies dormant — it was once on the market for a couple of million Euros. Like the ICC nearby or Tegel Airport, it could be transformed into something else like flats or a restaurant — just repaint it the original red.

A CARLESS FUTURE?

Extinction Rebellion supported the retention of the Ringway Centre and Birmingham's Smallbrook Queensway and I hope they and others will recognize this book not as a bone-headed celebration of our past profligacy with concrete or a get-out-of-jail-free card for the car and oil companies, but as something different. I hope drivers will also see I'm not totally trashing them, just gently rinsing them. This is really a tale of the times, of past times.

The present is a strange mishmash. The ubiquitous deep-orange high-vis vest that used to be associated with roadwork gangs now has a different meaning as Just Stop Oil protestors sit in the street, form slow convoys or take up positions on motorway gantries. Motorists get incensed, feeling that they are being objected to when it is really the oil companies, and that the whole thing is of course a publicity stunt (that clearly works in those terms). The message is heard, it must be. But there is a sense that the driver's world is closing in. They can't go where they want, when they want any more. Everyone is on their back — even the satnav moaning about taking the 'wrong' turn.

Car showroom,
A Coruña, Spain

A carless future then? Well, the answer is obviously 'no' to whether the future will be car-less, but not categorically. What we've seen in cities now is a feverish attempt to undo 50 years of planning. The plans of almost all large cities called for more and more roads, with roads to connect them to other cities. The future is going to have to be considerably greener if we are to survive and the planet is too. Some

changes have been easy, some have proved highly controversial. Low Traffic Neighbourhoods (LTNs) in Britain have tried to remove cars from residential streets. If it was your street you were in luck. If you lived on the street the excess traffic now had to travel down – well... The new streetscape of the LTN is planters blocking roads and empty tarmac. There has also been increased charging and tolls and an attempt to keep older, more-polluting vehicles out of cities. Whole freeways like the Minhocão in São Paulo are periodically turned over to pedestrians.

Wide roads have had cycle lanes and more pedestrian pavements added since Covid, fast roads have been slowed. Grade separation is as out of favour now as it was in favour in the 60s. Surface boulevards with crossings and tree-lined parklets are the future. We need to encourage walking and cycling, of course. The surface runoff from roads is literally killing our rivers. We need to sort out the mess and the pollution – driving is a dirty business. We will always travel; we must. But we cannot wreck everything as we do so. Let's celebrate the stylish designs of the past, let's try to understand the dramatic and weird designs the car age brought, let's accept it was dehumanizing but still see the power in it like writers Iain Sinclair and Chris Petit do. Let's look to the future and make things cleaner and greener and try to listen and learn.

UK

Preston Bus Station

Of the many post-war bus stations built in Britain, Preston stands out as probably the best. The Building Design Partnership offering is not perfect: it kind of sits apart from the town, and a recent refurbishment aimed to make it friendlier, more hospitable and more accessible. The previous subways and tunnels were a lowlight. However, the sweep of white car-park decks rightly became an iconic sight, a true classic of the era and a celebration of the bus — something you won't read very often. They flick upwards like a 60s quiff on a Teddy boy's head. Silhouetted against the sky, multi-storey car parks do have that ability to look more thrilling than they have any right to be. I was chucked out of this one when someone called security to moan at me for taking pictures on the roof. This is the perfect backdrop for Sarah Hardacre's art, where kitsch 60s pin ups are photomontaged against Northern British brutalism.

Markham Moor Services

(GB) MARKHAM MOOR, UK

I guess I've been researching this book since I was a kid, when so much of my time seemed to be spent on the A17 and the A1 between Norfolk and Yorkshire. The things that obsess the child, it seems, still obsess the adult. The highlight of that journey was the Markham Moor services, then a Little Chef, now a Starbucks, and originally a petrol station. This 1960 wonder by Hajnal-Kónyi and Sam Scorer is listed and protected because of its astonishing parabolic roof, a slice of California Googie in the English East Midlands. The Beauty of Transport blog compares its swooping roof to the TWA Flight Center at New York's JFK Airport. It is a *Mad Men* time capsule, for sure. In the 1990s it was a welcome sign of an Early Starter fry-up to fuel the rest of the journey to Bradford.

Margaret Calvert's Traffic Signs

Margaret Calvert's designs for Britain's traffic signs will be instantly recognizable to all residents of those weird islands. They are a triumph. The clarity and legibility of all these signs sing; they are one of the greatest pieces of modern graphic design. It's funny to see the same signs from the 1960s in photos when everything else looked so different. Calvert's inspirations were various: famously she and her brother inspired the School sign. Even the lettering on the British signs is brilliant. Britain may think it's the best and largely be wrong, but these signs probably are the best in the world. The pictograms look great, the words look great. At speed on a motorway they are supremely easy to read. Fashion designer Anya Hindmarch was inspired to create a collection based around them, and who remembers 1990s Britpop band Gay Dad – whose graphic designs were based on the lettering and the pedestrian-crossing man?

Leeds — Motorway City of the 70s

(GB) LEEDS, UK

Leeds was, as it boasted on postmarked letters, the 'Motorway City of the Seventies'. Perhaps someone somewhere in the city planning department was having a private joke with the motorway in question though — when you look on a map at the A58M/A64M Inner Ring Road designed to speed cars through Leeds, it takes on the unmistakable shape of... a snail.

The entire length of the snailway boasted a cornucopia of concrete, from the Yorkshire Post Building at the west end to Leeds Metropolitan University's Brunswick Building at the east end. The latter went in 2009 so Kaiser Chiefs could play bigger gigs at the new First Direct Arena that replaced it. There's no doubt about it: Leeds is sweeping away its 60s and 70s past.

The 1967 International Pool, with its imposing black roof, also got the chop in '09.

In City Square and around the Merrion Centre almost all traces of the impressively bonkers 1970s network of elaborate overhead pedestrian walkways and subways with their alfresco escalators are gone. The urban legends of what the council planned continue to obsess Loiners. Did the planners really want to renumber every floor level of every building in the city, with City Square being 1? Certainly Leeds University's Level 10 corridor is higher up the hill and students continue to be entranced by tales of sci-fi TV shows being filmed there, and of it being the longest corridor on Earth.

The Shopping Malls of Rodney Gordon and Owen Luder

(GB) UK

Owen Luder was, as they'd say in *Howards' Way*, 'an astute businessman' who knew how to get contracts signed. He inked deals to build massive shopping centres across Britain in places like Bath, Catford, Portsmouth and Gateshead. These were no ordinary shopping malls though. Because, despite the commercial mind of Luder, it was the design direction of the genius Rodney Gordon — one of the best brutalists — that elevated the works into a different level of complexity and panache. We know them latterly as down-at-heel — the Catford Centre's roof is eerie yet intriguing. It, like so many of the schemes, was mixed use — but the car was central. There were often flats on top, shops below, a market and the ubiquitous car park. The Tricorn (pictured) in Portsmouth was a *Gesamtkunstwerk*, which was obviously demolished by councillors. The Trinity in Gateshead had a rooftop café on top of the thin and elegant parking decks which featured so famously in the gangster movie *Get Carter*.

Ring Roads in the English Midlands

GB UK

As the heart of the British motor industry, it's unsurprising that the West Midlands is home to a number of elaborate ring roads. Wolverhampton has a tight dual-carriageway circuit (which homeless man Josef Stawinoga camped out on for three decades), while Stourbridge has a bizarre one-way ring road akin to a gigantic roundabout. Leicester has an over-engineered Inner Ring Road and a looooong outer one. Kidderminster has one which is almost, but not quite, complete.

Birmingham's famous Queensway (pictured being opened by HM Queen Elizabeth II on Apr 7, 1971), known as 'the concrete collar', is being slowly downgraded. Its labyrinthine Masshouse Circus junction was removed in 2002 to provide land for speculative property development. The Rotunda has survived on top of the old St Martin's Circus as a symbol of the car age in Brum. The battle in Birmingham now is to save the Smallbrook Ringway Centre, which curves along the southern side of the Queensway but which the council want to demolish. Now we know that although it was wasteful to build using so much concrete, we should save what we have rather than demolishing and rebuilding again.

Paradise Circus

Brum is an adorable oddball; an eccentric void at the centre of the nation and yet the centre of nothing. And at the centre of Birmingham: Paradise. (What a word!) A roundabout that defined the city with the library on top of it. Birmingham transforms. Birmingham forgets. Buildings, dreams and memories live in the same unreal world here. Birmingham Central Library was a dreamlike building: John Madin's fantasy made real. Sometimes it's hard to know where dreams end and reality begins. A few years ago on a return visit to this rabbit warren before it was finally demolished, I saw a child's abandoned toy pushchair out here in the broken water garden — just left, forgotten. That image will never leave me. Why was it there? Paradise Circus today boasts a warren of hidden squares, underground stairs, haunted passageways, dead ends. The scent of Nando's hung in the air as night fell. A busker played a lament on a saxophone. A thud behind me. Human or ghost? Reality or dream? The shape of a cyclist materialized from the darkness.

'D'you know how to get out of here?' he laughed.

YARMOUTH A143
MILDENHALL A1101
THETFORD A134
A 14 IPSWICH
A 14 STOWMARKET
A134 SUDBURY
F420

Remnants of the Early Years of Motoring

(GB) UK

Before anyone realized we were destroying the environment, and before the massive post-war take-up of cars, there was a world where motorways barely existed and the pace of life was more tranquil. But the coming of the car was still anticipated: Bury St Edmunds' chief architect Basil Oliver designed the art deco Pillar of Salt sign for the market town in 1935, its illuminated letters pointing drivers to Ipswich or Thetford. Meanwhile, if your Austin blew a gasket on the A45, you could look for help in the form of an AA or RAC box depending on which organization you were a member of. You'd get a key which unlocked the yellow or blue box and you could call from a phone inside before we all had mobiles. A handful of the AA boxes remain, such as Box 161 at Crickhowell in Powys on the A40, which has now been protected. Some 'pre-Worboys' (the committee that reported on standardization in 1963) signs still exist — especially in English villages. These are the historic signs that were used before Margaret Calvert's triumphant 1960s redesign of Britain's road signs.

Terry Farrell's Carchitecture

GB LONDON, UK

Before he made it big in China (very big) Terry Farrell whipped up some work in his native Britain which is highly pertinent to our little journey of discovery together. The first was two cracking ventilation shafts (this is one for Accidental Partridge, I fear) above the new Blackwall Tunnel built in the 1960s under the Thames. You can see them at Blackwall, standing almost like a mini-version of power station cooling towers — down the road from Goldfinger's Trellick Tower and right next to the point where the Smithsons' Robin Hood Gardens flats once stood — and these were also fitted with bespoke baffles to mitigate the effect of the East Cross Route dual carriageway, which runs past and then ducks under Farrell's follies. In the 1980s TVAM needed a new studio complex on a shoestring and chose a former car dealership and garage in Camden for the low-budget, high-effect job. Farrell paid a hundred quid each for the eggcups on the roof when the budget ran out and created a classic of post-modernism. Today the studio is still used for making TV by Paramount and MTV.

Tees Transporter

GB   MIDDLESBROUGH, UK

A transporter bridge, which carries a segment of roadway across a river, was judged the only suitable solution to the problem of letting tall-masted ships safely pass upriver to Stockton and the docks when Middlesbrough needed a new way to cross the Tees. But it would still have taken a leap of imagination and boldness to envisage building such a thing. What's seldom mentioned is the faith in the theories of modernism itself that the commissioners and builders of such structures would have had boiling in their veins.

Look at the list of where other transporter bridges were built: the first near Bilbao, others in Cheshire, one in South Wales, two more on the Elbe and the Kiel Canal in northern Germany, respectively. All (almost) uncrackable socialist heartlands; all embracing modernity in their chosen architecture. These bridges were suited to wide estuaries, and wide estuaries were also home to heavy industry and ports, and the people who worked in heavy industry and docking tended to be among the most left-leaning of all.

Over 250 metres (850ft) long, and painted in a distinctive royal blue that seemed to make the muddy Tees look even browner, the transporter was an instant monument.

British New Towns

(GB) UK

The Buckinghamshire New Town of Milton Keynes (pictured) is famous for its concrete cows, linear parks and listed Mies van der Rohe-inspired shopping centre. MK continues to be a pioneer — driverless cars recently hit its streets, and automated robotic buggies deliver shopping. When it was created in the 1960s and 70s the car was front and centre of the planners' minds. The city was split into grid squares with a neighbourhood inside each and main roads passing at the edges. There are of course so many roundabouts you'll go dizzy, but innovation too — the idea was to keep cars out of residential areas, and the Redway system allows bikes and pedestrians their own way round town. Roads run above the shopping centre in the middle allowing for deliveries and, although there are subways, they're not as scary as in some towns. Portes-cochere allow pedestrians to stay dry while walking through the city centre.

In Scotland, Cumbernauld came as an attempt to build a new type of city for the car age. The Scottish New Town, which dates from 1955, was immortalized in the classic 1981 romcom *Gregory's Girl*. Much of the action was set in the town centre designed by architect Geoffrey Copcutt — where all the town's shops, services, bus station, library and even flats sit in one enormous 'megastructure' with a fast highway passing beneath.

EUROPE

Bierpinsel

Stride up the steps from the fab U-Bahn station and you reach a whole new world that was supposed to be futuristic but is now crumbling like a stale cake. The primary-colour-pop modernity of the station gives way to the ground level of Steglitz's main shopping street, built when West Berliners lost access to the old city's centre. Shooting overhead is the highway overpass. Jog up the steps and you see the *chef d'oeuvre* of this crazy scheme — the Bierpinsel, or Beer Brush. It needs some tender loving care to restore it to its David Bowie heyday when the club here was quite the place to be. And it needs to be painted back into its bright-red original colour. It came on the market for a couple of million Euros a few years ago and I was very tempted to buy it (with a Kickstarter, of course) and move in here.

Novi Beograd

(SRB) BELGRADE, SERBIA

Fans of the wackiest brutalism are always looking for their new adventure. I generally point them in the direction of the former Yugoslavia – where Slovenia, Skopje and Serbia are all full of the most outré and exhilarating modernism, from *Spomeniks* to social-housing solutions. Novi Beograd (New Belgrade) is really concrete on acid. Tito-era redevelopment here was about socialist-minded housing for the people in huge *mikrorayons*, but also something more Western-focused too. The Western Gate Tower is a massive iconic monument next to the expressway running through the new city district of the Serbian capital. And even more transparent is the Sava Centar (not related to Sainsbury's brief hypermarket dalliance in the 1980s in the UK). This exhibition centre is designed for all kinds of businesses to meet in, contains bonkers sci-fi space-station interiors, has a glitzy hotel and, of course, parking for thousands of cars.

H-Day

One of the oddest episodes in road history occurred in 1967. While students around the world were protesting and hippies were dropping acid and dropping out, the government of Sweden preoccupied itself with an existential drama: switching sides of the road from left-hand to right-hand driving to match the neighbouring Nordic nations and indeed most of Europe — as it is really only Britain and Ireland that drive on the left around these parts.

Högertrafikomläggningen Day saw everyone switch sides on 3 September after an extensive preparation period of installing new signs, which were unveiled finally on the day. The overnight change caught the attention of the world's media who asked questions like: What the hell are you going to do with all the trams and buses with doors now on the wrong side? The answer: flog them to other left-hand countries in Asia. Panic and catastrophe was averted. One wonders what Ingmar Bergman made of all the fuss.

Lingotto Factory

(I) TURIN, ITALY

The Italy of the futurists and the white-hot modernism of a new industrial world made its presence felt in a corner of Turin that will forever be associated with the dynamism of the car. The Lingotto factory went up in the 1920s as a symbol of a thrusting new nation that was looking to the future. The highpoint was the rooftop test track, banked, incomparable to anything anywhere else in the world, a place where cars could speed round in the sky; a taste of the future. This was the FIAT factory where cars were manufactured and then could be run round at speed on the roof. It was a kind of European answer to River Rouge — Henry Ford's all-in-one factory complex at Dearborn, near Detroit. But Lingotto made everything vertical as if out of a futurist cartoon. It later featured in *The Italian Job*.

Autobahnüberbauung Schlangenbader Strasse

(D) BERLIN, GERMANY

West Berlin was so pressed for space that it had to come up with new ideas. Remember, the Berlin Wall encircled this city state and there was no room to expand outside it. Plans for Rolling Pavements and the Smithsons' own vision for a 3D West Berlin were discussed in my book, *Unbuilt*. One thing that made it to the real world though was The Snake. This stretched social-housing block straddles the former A104, now the ABZ Steglitz — a branch from the A100 Ring. It was the same kind of idea that Paul Rudolph had for enclosing and building on the LOMEX in New York. Flats here seem almost unaware that the road runs beneath. Well, things have changed latterly because now there is no traffic. Oh dear — some serious engineering failings have been found in the two road tunnels under the block. The road is closed for repairs until 2029. The scenario has a parallel in Chicago where the Eisenhower Expressway punches through the base of the Old Post Office.

Meriadeck

(F) BORDEAUX, FRANCE

I was alerted to this concoction by Jonathan Meades, who lived near Bordeaux before relocating to Le Corbusier's Unite in Marseille. The Bordeaux countryside was too bland for him — Meriadeck was not. It featured in one of his *Jonathan Meades on France* BBC TV essays, specifically the Caisse d'Epargne bank, a brutalist spaceship apparently sent to Earth in Aquitaine. The Meriadeck district was a mid-century *Alphaville* idea inspired by Colin Buchanan's grade-separation dogma where pedestrians had to be on podia up above vehicles. It shares a style with La Défense in Paris, parts of Birmingham and the dystopian double-level Lower Grand Avenue in Downtown LA where *The Terminator* was filmed. Meriadeck's platform sits above the main roads, with escalators up and down to the road, a shopping mall, interesting cruciform blocks including more than one hotel, a park and of course this bank. At night it's all so sci-fi and so far removed from the picture-postcard views of the classical city that tourists come for.

Austria's High Roads

(A) AUSTRIA

Austria has dozens of high roads, which are on many drivers' bucket lists. Chances are if you go road-tripping in Austria, you'll be asked if you've driven the Grossglockner Road, one of the most legendary high-pass trips in the Alps. With a bumper 36 turns and numerous steep inclines, this is a drive that will test your skills and the handling abilities of your car — make sure you have a good one, and plenty of tread on your tyres. You'll want to stop along the way to marvel at the views, especially the ones towards the Grossglockner, Austria's highest mountain at 3,798 metres (12,500ft). This snow-capped beast looks majestic at any time of year, as do the verdant valleys which sit below it. Many of the stopping points along the route make great stops for picnics, with elemental views of mountains, forests and sky. Hacked through the mountains in 1935, the road winds its way from Heilingenblut in Carinthia to Bruck near Salzburg. Start out early in the day to beat the rush — it can get pretty crowded up here in summer. And check the snow reports, as fresh falls can often close the road to traffic.

Faroes Tunnels

(FO) FAROE ISLANDS

The one corner of Europe I'd encourage everyone to visit, the Faroes defy the waffle of travel journalism prose. Their monumental seascapes are a clash: of land and water, of people and the elements, and of people and wildlife. The gallant topography of vertical cliffs on which puffins nest is cut through with mighty fjords, and this harsh terrain dominated life for centuries. The only way around was by sea. And even when roads came you still had to use ferries to fill in the gaps. In the last 50 years a big bath of Danish money has been lavished on challenging these landscapes with tunnels that cross the seas and link the tiny towns. They cancel the need for countless ferries and give the (wrong) impression that it's just one island. One even has a roundabout in it deep under the cold Norwegian Sea, unique in road tunnels.

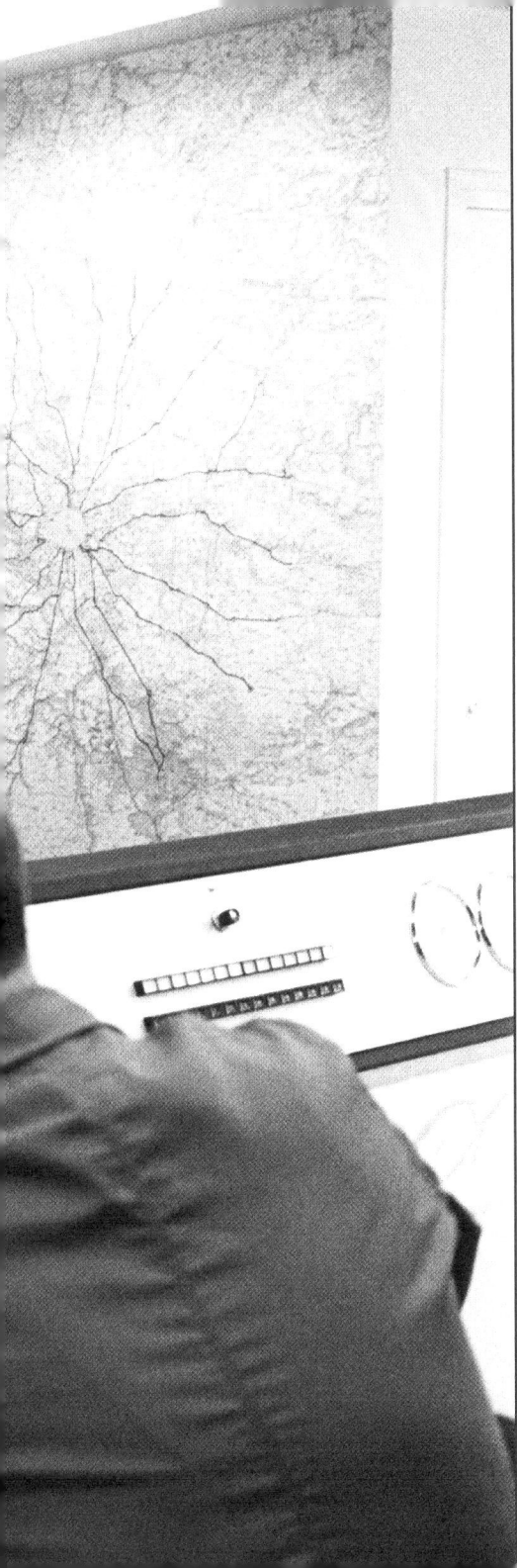

Périphérique

(F) PARIS, FRANCE

The super-tight circuit that encircles Paris exactly around its real geographic border like a belt around a pair of trousers, the Périphérique is a stressful drive, the busiest road in France. It took from 1958 to 1973 to build because of the disruption to city districts – but Paris achieved the inner motorway ring that London could only dream of and ended up scrapping with only a couple of bits finished. The technological and engineering brutality of the Périphérique inspired J.G. Ballard, but has left others cold – especially those who live outside of it and feel like second-class Parisians. Thus, in recent times the direction has been to cover bits over to recreate connections and try to follow green-leaning mayor Anne Hidalgo's mission to reduce the primacy of the car. This reached its apogee during the 'green games' of the 2024 Olympics. Paris was turned into a pedestrian friendly village and won worldwide plaudits. It's still staggering to think that anyone in a city as historic as Paris would have permitted this destruction for the Périphérique, but then during *Les Trente Glorieuses* after the Second World War anything was possible – La Défense brought a modern business district with plenty of parking and the numerous exurban estates of the period have bold architecture – from la Cité Picasso to les Choux de Creteil to the whole New Town district at Ivry jacked up above the road level and featuring dizzying star patterns.

Eastern Bloc Petrol Stations

(UA) (SLO) (RO) UKRAINE, SLOVENIA, ROMANIA

Kyiv's iconic 'Japanese Petrol Station' (of which there were two in the Ukraine capital in USSR days) lives on in the numerous shares of its wacky aesthetic on socials and in books. Any Soviet watcher immediately knows this quirky form with its dangling pumps and inevitable coterie of Ladas, Skodas and Tatras below. In Ljubljana, a new city was built, with classy modernist touches, in the Tito era. Its petrol stations and garages are standouts. The mushroom roof of the 1968 garage behind the Intercontinental at Tivolska 46 is a real eye-catcher. The always-interesting Spomenik Database website dug up the architect info: it was Milan Mihelič and engineer Jože Jaklič. Literally across the street is another petrol station with a skinny roof, almost Googie, with the kind of swoop of the TWA Center wings or the Markham Moor services. In Romania the state-owned PECO company was doing a natty job of building wacky modernist gas stations around the country and convincing people that it was modernizing.

fotopub
festival sodubne fifográfije v Nuvem mestú

Roundabout Art

(GB) (E) (P) (F)   UK, SPAIN, PORTUGAL, FRANCE

You might do a double take approaching the Dotterel roundabout near Reighton in Yorkshire because it looks from afar as if there are sheep grazing on it. Approaching, you quickly realize it's just another baaaarmy artwork — roundabouts in recent times have been taken over by all kinds of sculptures from the silly to the sublime. Honestly, most of them are crap, but there is fun to be had: in France, the huge kiwi in two halves on the Peyrehorade—Bayonne road in Nouvelle-Aquitaine, or the giant chair of Hagetmau. Jean-Luc Plé sounds like a made-up name for an artist, but he is responsible for the paper boats of La Tremblade and the legendary snail on the Lorignac roundabout, whose speed drivers would do well to ape.
A replica of the 1960s Aerotrain sits on a roundabout at Gometz-la-Ville. In Portugal there seems to be a proliferation of these sculptures around Sesimbra, with all kinds of boats and knights on roundabouts. For the best examples, head to Lanzarote, where César Manrique's sculptures trump all other roundabout art across the globe. These works are potent and starred in the Almodóvar classic *Broken Embraces*.

AMERICAS

Temple Street Parking Garage and Pirelli Building

(USA) NEW HAVEN, USA

New Haven is famous for Yale University. And Paul Rudolph's Art & Architecture Faculty Building is a classic of academic brutalism. But that modernist thread continues throughout the town; it is not just quads and courtyards and gardens. The same architect is responsible for the Temple Street garage, a car park that expresses optimism and is designed with flair and class – this is not an afterthought. It adds something to the town with its rigour and structure. The decks look like they belong and the concrete is deployed with panache. On the outskirts of town Marcel Breuer designed swish offices for Armstrong Rubber that are also full of vim. IKEA later bought the site and developed a store next door, leaving it empty for years. But now the Hotel Marcel has brought a high-end design hotel into the building, restoring its original details and celebrating this architecture and this age.

Brasilia

(BR)   BRAZIL

The new capital of Brazil was built so quickly — no lengthy public enquiries or ecological studies here — that the end result is of course questionable. It was derided as a 'ceremonial slum' by Robert Hughes, but he hated planners and this is a planner's dream come true. Built for the coming car age with the most monumental express roads, some are separated by huge medians whose width borders on the ridiculous. The Eixo Monumental is the kicker — a massive avenue of two halves with a central reservation that is beyond belief. It cuts down the centre of the city. Never pedestrian-friendly, a recent Metro has improved life for walkers. Nevertheless, as icons of modernism the buildings of Niemeyer and the plans and parks and bird-inspired top view of the city dreamed up by Costa and Burle Marx have created a capital which is unique and instantly recognizable. It is singular and it did its job of catapulting Brazil into the modern world.

America's Roadside Oddities

As a child I was captivated by a book given to me by my maternal grandmother which detailed a whole series of things you could see along America's long interstate freeways. Of course, there were the obvious stops like Mount Rushmore and the Civil War battlefields, but there was more eccentric material too, like big, strange sculptures and kooky stores that Denise Scott Brown picked out in her Proto-Pomo classic tome *Learning from Las Vegas* and termed 'ducks'. The Teapot Dome gas station in Washington State or the Big Fish Supper Club in Minnesota. Or how about Lucy the giant elephant in New Jersey. The Longaberger Basket Building in Ohio and the Beagle Motel in Idaho have since been added to this list and have captured the imagination of contemporary architectural adventurers like the great Rolando Pujol, who documents this quirky past and is interviewed in this book.

Motels

Perhaps the most distinctive of the American mid-century hotels is Roy's, on the old Route 66, in the desert not too far out from Joshua Tree. The arrow on the sign means business; the fact that it's not surrounded by endless, listless strip-mall development, but stands alone, adds a cinematic potency. The Starlite Motel (pictured overleaf) in Kerhonkson uses its big red sign and pink paint to lure Brooklyn hipsters up to the Catskills. The Quail Park Lodge in Utah has a natty blue sign that pulls in travellers and sings of the 60s. The Trixie Motel in Palm Springs is a peach, likewise the Pearl in San Diego. There are dozens more of these heritage motels across the country, their poppy palettes and retro signs an antidote to the crass commercialization of the country.

Miami Beach Parking Structures

(USA) MIAMI, USA

Miami Beach — famous for fun, sun, swimsuits, salacious Art Basel parties, Scarface, slick architecture… and now car parks too. Miami Beach has taken what many cities see as an eyesore or something to be ashamed of and elevated them. Its multi-level parking garages are designed by famous architects and have become bizarre attractions in their own right. 1111 Lincoln Road Garage is by Swiss supremos Herzog & de Meuron and boasts skinny struts and wafer-like decks, but there are numerous other aesthetically pleasing examples too. There's a Frank Gehry garage on Pennsylvania Avenue, though a planned Zaha Hadid car park was never completed in the end. It's apt that so many rich *American Psycho*-esque types (they've probably not read the book) power up and down the beachfront road in their souped-up motors. And now they have somewhere cool to park them while they're at the shops or by the beach or visiting their mistress.

Minhocão

A road that has become more than just a piece of infrastructure, but something with cultural significance like the Westway or the 101 or Le Périphérique, this São Paulo elevated highway even has its own bizarre moniker: Minhocão — a mythical 'big worm'. We can laugh up to a point, but it's obviously no joke if your window is five metres from the carriageway. The road has latterly become famous for *not* being a piece of carchitecture. Fed-up residents have managed to get it closed on nights and weekends, when it becomes a playground, park and cycle track. Perhaps its future lies here with no automobile traffic, to be reimagined rather like Seoullo 7017 — the former flyover made into an urban park in the South Korean capital. São Paulo has many other expressways: one slices right downtown through Sé, another features legendary murals by Os Gemeos (The Twins).

Marina City

Chicago famously kept its overhead railways, to maintain a downtown defined by rails rather than roads — unusual in North America. But the modern era didn't pass by. Mies van der Rohe built his Lake Shore Drive apartments squarely with the car-driving condo-owner in his sights. And next to his IBM Building is something else. Right here is Marina City by Bertrand Goldberg — two corncobs of flats that stand as proud as pie, with docks for boats by the river and car entry ramps from street level, two floors higher up. There's then spiral parking decks with the flats levitating above the auto area. They're simple, cheap, organic structures. They look like they grew from the ground. They were built in 1964 and were a very early attempt at the regeneration we see everywhere in cities from New York to Norwich. So although they were car-friendly, they were meant to tempt the middle classes away from the rapidly burgeoning suburbs and back to the city centre. Yes you will recognise them from the cover of Wilco's alt-folk album Yankee Hotel Foxtrot.

Los Angeles

Reyner Banham said Los Angeles 'makes nonsense of history and breaks all the rules' in his brilliant 1972 documentary where he drives the city. There is nowhere like this sprawling, sleazy, exciting and sometimes frustrating metropolis, where the car is king and distances between sights are eye-watering (a rush-hour trip from Venice to Downtown can take almost two hours). LA has soul, it's a city like a country with millions of new immigrants and dreamers from around the world trying to make it in the movies or in life. Celluloid is the *sine qua non* of LA: a visit to Warner Brothers Studios is essential and you can see the places where countless movies were shot, like *Drive*. Mulholland Drive is one of the most famous streets — David Lynch fans don't need to be told why. The Four Level Interchange is listed as a national monument and dates from way back in the 1940s. The Arroyo Seco Parkway runs north to Pasadena — one of the earliest freeways in the US. Its kitschy lamps and bridges make it seem like something from Disneyworld. Freeway City is gridlocked half the time; you hear people talk about parking in every conversation, about the '10' and the '101' as if they're people. No wonder the police have so many helicopters. Santa Monica is the end of Route 66, the destination, the dream — one you drive to, natch.

Southern California Banks

The architectural highlight of Southern California may well be its banks. Sometimes aping European modernism (Ronchamp roof, anyone?) they are true mid-century classics. The best collection of the modernist banks are in Palm Springs, where there's a cluster built with car parks for the new arrivals whose suburban villas were a few miles drive from the downtown area. Rudy Baumfield's Bank of America (pictured) is pure kitsch. Opposite is E. Stewart Williams' Chase Bank, which may or may not owe a debt to Oscar Niemeyer. On Sunset and Vine in Hollywood, Millard Sheets' Home Savings & Loan from 1968 is eye-catching and also boasts a mural and a fountain out front, and on the opposite corner is a brutalist monster Bank of America that you won't be able to stop staring at either. After these came drive-thru banks once ATM technology meant you didn't need to go inside any more. The website Roadside Architecture (www.roadarch.com) has a comprehensive list of all the California modernist banks if you want to do a tour — and you should.

Fordlandia

BR   BRAZIL

Henry Ford had grand plans. His River Rouge plant at Dearborn was more like a city than a factory, its non-union hellishness so noteworthy that it would end up being studied by me in sociology class at university 80 years later. Ford would have been happy that he even got an 'ism' named after him. He liked everything big. Having conquered Michigan he set his sights on Brazil and the grand plan for a factory and whole new city in the Amazon jungle. Ostensibly built to source rubber for his cars' tyres, Fordlandia could also be the playground where he lived out his city-planner dreams. That dream faded; the city in the jungle still exists, but as a kind of memento mori. Ford also developed other huge factories around the world, like the massive Dagenham plant by the Thames in Essex.

Ed Ruscha Paintings

USA | USA

If J.G. Ballard was the poet laureate of the auto age, Ed Ruscha was the court artist. His paintings picked at the scabs of the moral shortcomings of the new isolated world we would explore behind the wheel, often alone. But they also reflected the dynamism of the newly moving world, where things and people didn't stand still – where bleakness and optimism somehow mixed. The modernity here was a corporate one: everything is specified with signs and brands: a Ford badge, the Standard Station. His 1964 work, *Norm's La Cienega, On Fire*, asks as many questions about the era as it answers – was it predicting the tumbling of the American Dream five short years from when it was painted? Andy Warhol was obsessed with advertising and consumerism; Ruscha picks on the words and their sounds especially. *Honk* is easy enough to understand. If Edward Hopper's *Nighthawks* distilled the American urban experience of the 1940s into one image then Ruscha's works perhaps did the same for a decade where previous mores were blown apart and the individualism that the car represented meant that a million different routes through life were suddenly becoming possible.

Drive-thrus

(USA)   USA

How could we forget the thing by the roadside that brings us the most joy. Yes, roads are bad, and yes, cars are polluting, and yes, fast food is a disaster for the planet — read *Fast Food Nation* and you may never want to stop for a burger ever again. But at the same time, there is something of the kid in us that can't resist. We can't be perfect all the time, and for those times there is the drive-thru. It's also obvious that on some journeys you simply need to eat and drink. The quirky designs of the drive-thru lure us in with logos and colours as if we were still children. The best of the mass-market chains is In-N-Out — their regulation design includes the twin palm trees and eye-catching yellow flash logo. But connoisseurs seek out the independents, like the Donut Hole. Soon every brand wanted a drive-thru and there is scarcely a restaurant that doesn't offer them today. And it's not just food — drive-thru banking, laundry, film development... you name it, Americans will not get out of their cars to do it.

WORLDWIDE

Tiny Homes with Car Parking

(J) JAPAN

In a country where space is tight and technology drives social change, it was inevitable that architects would turn their hands to designing the tiniest possible house — with, of course, space to park. The iconic tiny house is Yasuhiro Yamashita's Reflection of Mineral in Tokyo. Its shape immediately makes you think of a crystal and it includes — naturally — space to park a VW Beetle. A three-storey slightly less tiny house by APOLLO Architects also comes with its requisite car port as the first floor perches above your motor. Now the ante has been upped and designers are dreaming up even smaller houses that are literally the size of a parking space.

Australia's Big Things

Weird, wacky, impossible to understand, distracting, never ending, a lot of cheap drama made for not a lot of bucks. Yes, TV's *Neighbours* is quite something. Oh. But you came here for the Big Things right? A bonkers notion that gained so much traction that today there are dozens of the damn things around the country, the Big Things were there to lure passing motorists, especially when new highway bypasses were being built from the 1960s onwards — and to encourage small-town meanders rather than big-brand 'servo' stops. The most famous is the Big Banana in Coff's Harbour. But you'd be remiss not to stop for the Big Prawn, the Big Merino, the Big Beer Can, the Big Orange and all the others. Also check out the Big Bowl in Lake Cathie, which celebrates the sport beloved of Australia's seniors. And the Big Crab in Miriam Vale.

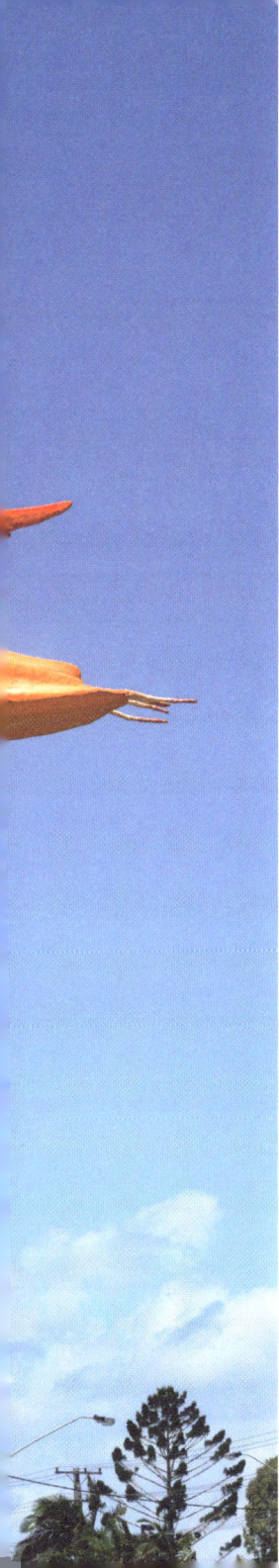

Tel Aviv Bus Station

'What are you going to do today?' a friend asked me in Tel Aviv.

'Visit the bus station!'

They looked aghast. No wonder. It is a warren of passageways and flyovers in the sky connecting either the world's biggest or second biggest (depending on how you measure it) bus station to the expressways out of town. There are bomb shelters, cheap eats, shops selling flip-flops, and people just hanging around. It is, though, an amazing megastructure dreamed up in 1967 at the height of such monolithic visions and is an insight into how we saw ourselves, our cities and our transport needs back in those pot-smoking days. Designed by Ram Karmi, it was altered many times and only completed two decades after he initially thought it up; the world had changed — but you still get your bus from here. There's another intriguing example from this era at Atarim Square, where the beach expressway is funnelled under this mid-century mixed-plaza, which has a public deck, an inverted ziggurat building housing a hotel, and plenty of ramps, stairs and underground nooks and crannies — it's not too far removed from Paradise Circus in Birmingham, weirdly.

Hill Road Flyover

(HK) HONG KONG, CHINA

It's a surprise to find how many highways have been threaded through Hong Kong. Navigating these and the confusing overhead walkways that meander above them is not always easy, but they are a part of this unique cityscape. The most famous surgical intervention into the topography of the former colony is Hill Road in Shek Tong Tsui. The flyover was opened in 1981 as an on-ramp to link Hong Kong University and the buildings halfway up the hill to the northern coast motorway, running along by the sea. The flyover therefore trundles along between old buildings some seven or so floors up in the air and seems bizarre in photos. Recently a new city park was installed under the flyover to create a more liveable space for nearby residents. The flyover shares perhaps some DNA with the Mid-Levels Escalator — another techie transport system which moves people rather than cars up the steep hills of Hong Kong.

Tashkent

(UZ) UZBEKISTAN

Rebuilt after the Second World War to be the capital of Soviet Asia, Tashkent was expanded and altered, and naturally the Soviet triumphal avenue plan was put to work in the same way as in East Berlin, Halle-Neustadt, Minsk and numerous other examples. They said it was to provide quicker journeys and prepare cities for the car age – but there was an ulterior motive. As with Baron Haussmann's Paris boulevards, so avenues are easier to manage and dominate than old warrens of streets; they impose the most top-down order and are also perfect for military parades. Some buildings from this era include the famous Circus and the Hotel Uzbekistan (set on the side of a huge roundabout really), and the Tashkent Modernism group are preserving and promoting these buildings – not always easy when anything 'communist' is almost always loathed and ripe for replacement, as can be seen most spectacularly in Skopje, which has turned from metabolist hotbed to Vegas-esque fever dream.

Kings Cross Junction

(AUS) SYDNEY, AUSTRALIA

Having spent a bit of time walking around this area, I suppose I've come to think of this junction as a kind of Times Square or Piccadilly Circus of Australia. There's the multiple roads meeting and the big-scale advertising: the thing that stands out most in Kings Cross is the huge Coca-Cola board, lit up at night and advertising not just the soda but the dubious attractions of 'The Cross', a questionable yet fun spot in a city that is too obsessed with cleaning itself up. The massive apartment block used to be a Hyatt when the new road tunnel was smashed through as part of a route from Sydney's Central Business District to the beaches and the Eastern Suburbs; the memory of drunk sailors and the heroine Juanita Nielsen, a feisty female journalist who took on the mob here and deserves a statue — it all bubbles to the surface.

Asmara

ER ASMARA, ERITREA

To caveat this entry, the Italian takeover here was fraught and bloody, and I fully recognize the tyranny of all colonization. Yet some of the architectural memories we have from that era are worth close investigation. The development of Asmara as a modern city influenced by futurist ideals could not have been possible without the focus on the fetish of the new automobiles. Dozens of buildings bear witness to this time, none more startling than the Fiat Tagliero garage with its trademark wings, which locals didn't believe would stay up. In the *Guardian*, Edward Denison tells the story of when the architect Giuseppe Pettazzi attended the opening: 'at the building's unveiling, Pettazzi is said to have put a gun to the contractor's head and ordered him to remove the supports'. Charming.

The Gate

OSAKA, JAPAN

A classic case of 'owner would not sell up' creating a drama in the same way as the farm in the middle of the M62 in Yorkshire or the house in the way of the expressway in China. Here in Osaka we have a 70m-tall office tower with a road running right through a hole in the middle of it. The Expressway Company opted to continue with the endeavour rather than rerouting, creating something singular. The road apparently does not touch the building, the tower has floors missing and the two just get on with both their lives. Japan went crazy for these urban expressways, and they're often elevated too — the way they thread through the skies above the streets of Tokyo is impressive but also hair-brained. It's confusing, but a drive along them feels like a big adventure. For pedestrians, maybe it's not quite so good.

Motorway Art

Apartheid-era Johannesburg was disgracefully segregated but economically on a roll. The white government wanted to expand and modernize their cities on the American model, and Johannesburg is essentially the New York of southern Africa. The M1 motorway was built right through the city on a north—south axis and several mansions in Parktown were sacrificed on the altar of progress. The pillars beneath the flyovers in Newtown found a new life as the canvas for street art, likewise the sides of warehouses facing what is probably South Africa's busiest road. Street art has become a big deal in the city. The motorway also came at a time when Jo'burg was building other structures that seemed apt for the age, like the concrete Carlton Centre in the CBD (Central Business District) and the infamous Ponte City Tower in Hillbrow — whose up-and-down story deserves a film and whose dystopian interiors will no doubt be familiar to you from a lot of Instagram posts.

Supermarkets

The supermarket was the corollary of the car. Now you could go grocery shopping for everything you needed in one place, in one go. The brutalist GEM in Sens, France, by Claude Parent from 1970 is an explosion of jagged shapes and optimism. Rather more grounded British versions from the following decade always evoked a farm. These silly Disney-fied kind of post-modern brick behemoths on the edges of towns like King's Lynn featured barnyard whimsy, clock towers and cock weathervanes, and a café where the jacket potatoes were never bad – and the petrol was cheap too. Nevertheless, havoc was wreaked on the high streets of small towns by the new superstores. Some inner-city supermarkets stand out – especially the high-tech Camden Sainsbury's by Nicholas Grimshaw from 1988, which looks thoroughly robotic and has a great hot food selection. Each supermarket came with a massive car park. And of course the branding, the lights, the logo and the sign: the edges of towns around the world were decorated with Carrefour, Pingo Doce, Mercadona, IGA, Trader Joe's, Coles, Chedraui, Rewe, Morrisons and Aldi plumage.

Airports Built for Cars

USA) (D) KANSAS CITY AND BERLIN

For TWA's hub at Kansas City the 'Drive to the Gate' philosophy reigned supreme. It was 1972 of course, perhaps the peak year of motorway madness, when driving was the panacea and the oil crisis was just over the horizon. Brochures advertised the 25-metre (75ft) walk from kerbside to aircraft, achieved by building long and thin curving terminals with access roads stretched out in front of them. In West Berlin two years later the same idea was pressed into service at Tegel, the new airport for the enclave. Here the terminal was a giant hexagon (and indeed this motif is continued everywhere in the striking 'total' design). Again roads went right in front of each building and the idea was to drive your car right up to the airport and walk almost nowhere — no 10,000-steps-a-day worries back then! Naturally both ideas ran into huge problems when you had to insert numerous security screening points, but nevertheless Tegel especially is a brutalist bobby-dazzler.

Cars on Film

Hollywood (and its worldwide corollaries) barely bothered with trains, trams and metros after World War II. The focus was always on cars: *The Italian Job*, *Get Carter*, *Weekend*, *Wild Strawberries*. *Easy Rider* put motorbikes in the frame. Godard's *Alphaville* was a dystopian wonder. Ballard's *Crash* was late to the table after its publication in 1973 as a novel, yet David Cronenberg's 1996 treatment is intriguing. The biggest shame is that Ballard's *Concrete Island* is yet to be filmed, and that it was not made in the 1970s – the era it belongs in. I wonder sometimes what a celluloid version would look like and why it has yet to appear.

The road movie is one of cinema's most satisfying genres – *Elizabethtown*, *Little Miss Sunshine*, *Y Tu Mamá También*, *The Trip*. My novel *The Wall in the Head* was partly an attempt to do a 'road movie novel', paying homage to the car-crazy brutalist era. Wim Wenders' road movies are the greatest – and he gets trains in too: *Alice in the Cities*, *Kings of the Road* and *Paris, Texas* (pictured) take film-making beyond the dead-dull 'two people sat in a room talking' model that sabotages so many scripts. Christopher Petit cheekily gave his script for *Radio On* to Wenders when he interviewed him as a journalist, and Wenders agreed to produce. *Radio On* is the greatest British road movie, with guest turns from Sting, the Westway and Bristol's Redcliffe Flyover.

Tunnel Renaissance — Burying Roads

USA   IRL   D   BOSTON, SEATTLE, DUBLIN, HAMBURG

In J.G. Ballard's biting satire *Concrete Island*, architect Robert Maitland ploughs his Jaguar off the M4 and wakes up trapped within a tangle of slip roads. The novel was published in 1974, when motorways were all the rage. But that dystopian vision of chunky flyovers and tangled roads in the sky is disappearing, as cities around the world are electing to hide roads down in the ground.

Boston's 'Big Dig' megaproject took 20 years to put the city's main elevated freeway in a tunnel, and Seattle did exactly the same. Hamburg is also sending its roads underground, and it wants to go even further and get rid of all cars from the centre of the city. Meanwhile, Sydney has built a brand-new road tunnel right under the centre of town. But it doesn't come cheap — Boston's tunnel was over budget by 200 per cent, coming in at an eye-watering £10bn. Dublin's Port Tunnel looks like a snip in comparison, at £500m.

Tunnels remove noise and pollution; they give us space. Conspiracy theorists might spy an ulterior motive, though. When the motorways were built above ground in all these cities in the 1950s, land was cheap and urban living was seen as second-best. Now neither is true, and the space freed up for blocks of flats will make a fortune for a lucky few. (If the artists' impressions are to be believed, there will also be attractive new public parks for the rest of us.)

Bridges

The age of roads meant that motorways needed to go where it was believed that they would never be able to go. Rivers and even seas needed to be crossed. Ferries had been enough before, but not now. This necessitated a great new era of bridge building that kicked off with the Golden Gate in San Francisco and reached its apotheosis with previously unthinkable crossings like Oresund Crossing between Copenhagen and Malmo (pictured overleaf) or the 17km (10½-mile) Vasco de Gama bridge in Lisbon. Few can match the 55km (34-mile) bridge between Hong Kong and Macau that has captivated many onlookers. Some of the bridges are beautiful, like the spindly Kylesku Bridge in Sutherland which curves elegantly on its skinny struts. Some bridges make us feel small, like the 340m-high Millau Viaduct (pictured) by Norman Foster, which carries a motorway across the Millau Gorge in southern France and is so high the clouds swirl around its deck and the local birds are undoubtedly *un petit peu* confused. And some are just weird: the UFO Bridge (pictured overleaf) in Bratislava is a communist-era icon that splits opinion with its saucer observation deck on top.

Malls

In the US the mall is a story of rise and fall — just like that of car culture really. The emerging suburbs and the 'lazy decades' led to the mega-mall being built on the outskirts of cities. I remember very well my first mall — and how difficult it was to walk there. Dearborn's mall brought to mind the comedy of Kevin Smith, whose movies like *Mallrats* and *Clerks* lashed out at the vapid stupidity of consumer culture. The mall punters are zombies in a way, clutching Orange Julius and JCPenney bags. But teenagers come to goof around and flirt too. The malls spread around the world. In Britain the names conjure shopaholism — Meadowhall, the Metro Centre. In Eastern Europe, South America and Asia the malls are still spreading, as consumerism isn't as toxic as it has become in the West. And there is less desire for the kind of 'market' nostalgia that has taken over as we seek a simpler life with a softer, more individual, hipster capitalism at its heart. In the US, malls have closed, city centres have become more popular, online shopping now of course reigns supreme, and a new laziness has taken over too — rather than plodding mall corridors, people want to park outside big box stores, which are a new typology that has spread, with IKEAs and everything else, on busy road junctions outside of cities. City-centre malls from the 1960s, like Bradford's Arndale, are still a kitsch pleasure though.

ESSAYS

The Kelpies, Scotland

SUPER-SIZED SCULPTURES BY THE ROADSIDE

The Kelpies are an intriguing pair of giant horse heads in Falkirk that make any car journey up the M9 infinitely more interesting. At 30m (98ft) tall and weighing 300 tonnes, they are the largest equine sculptures on Earth.

Britain likes it big. And we have many sculptures next to major roads. But, for the council committees commissioning them, is it more about rebranding a place than a love of art?

'I'm not entirely sure,' says Andy Scott, the affable sculptor of The Kelpies. 'It's a hell of a risky way to rebrand. Any council or civic authority would have to be very certain that it would work in their favour.'

Public art is mainstream now, but it hasn't always been the norm. The monument that shifted attitudes was Antony Gormley's *Angel of the North*, which opened in 1998 and became both a symbol of the Northeast and of how Britain finally fell for sculpture. Like The Kelpies, it was placed next to a major road where every day thousands of people would pass by and see it.

Sheffield had its Tinsley cooling towers, which it blew up. These sat next to the M1 Tinsley Viaduct and were a symbol of the Don Valley. Tower blocks and industrial structures have become unfashionable. They lack the touristy sheen that image-conscious British towns of today want. Yet Antony Gormley loves a cooling tower. He told the BBC's *Omnibus* in 2000, 'Something like that is incredibly inspiring. It's better than a cathedral.'

Big sculpture has a long history. 'The construction of large public sculpture has always been there, from the Ancient Egyptians to the present day,' says Peter Murray, founding director of the Yorkshire Sculpture Park, home to a flock of Henry Moores. As with many observers, Murray wants more art and less PR from this wave of British megastructures: 'What I hope for is a greater concern with scale, artistic context and integrity, rather than [sculpture as] a means of promoting regeneration.' There was at one time a plan to build a giant horse by Mark Wallinger next to the A2 at Ebbsfleet. In the US the Enchanted Highway in North Dakota contains many oversized scrap-metal sculptures by Gary Greff.

Birmingham is the latest city on the hunt for a super-sized sculpture. It already has a giant Gormley of its own, *Iron:Man*. But Gormley fell out with the city fathers after saying in the same *Omnibus* film that: 'I think [Victoria] Square is appalling, a monument to Thatcherite Britain… it was very, very important to me that I made something that had absolutely nothing to do with that kind of shit.'

Despite this disconnect between civic showing-off and artistic temperament, Brum has been mulling a return for Nic Munro's giant pop-art *King Kong*. A film ostensibly about punk band The Nightingales but which features *King Kong* heavily was made by Stewart Lee and Michael Cumming, charting its journey from the old Bull Ring in 1972 to a farm in Penrith. In 2022 a copy was placed next to Soho Road in Birmingham.

Angel of The North, UK

RING ROAD POETS
OF COVENTRY

Encircling an eccentric city centre where medieval streets meet the modern world, this hulking piece of 1970s infrastructure is the subject of 27 poetry films celebrating its bizarre concrete beauty

The urban landscape has long set literary imaginations on fire — but a ring road may not spring to mind as an obvious source of poetic inspiration. In Coventry, however, the overt orbicular oddness of the ring road and its nine junctions, each elbowing the city, has been celebrated in a collaborative homage to concrete and tarmac by nine poets and nine film-makers.

'The ring road reminds me of a huge creature,' mulls Leanne Bridgewater, one of the poets involved in the Disappear Here project, dreamed up by local artist Adam Steiner.

'The ring road has a great presence, not dissimilar to the old city walls,' reflects Steiner, 'but driving on it reminds me of Scalextric!' The roller-coaster qualities of driving the road are legendary — you can complete the circuit in five minutes.

The story of post-war planning in the UK is often one of false starts and half finishes. Coventry is one of the few places that actually followed through, with its new city centre and ring road completed in 1974. Seen from above, the city is as circular as a dart board. But you'd have to be a sober shot to hit the bullseye — as its equally circular ring road is tightly drawn around the city

Conventry Ring Road

centre, creating a remarkable urban landscape.

Within that tight circle lies one of the most architecturally fascinating city centres in Britain, where medieval streets meet the modern world. The mild modernism of Coventry's immediate post-war rebuild has much in common with cities that suffered similar fiery fates, such as Essen and Rotterdam.

The style of its shopping centre is Scandinavian, mixed with a little of Chester's influence in the double-decker streets. The western section of ring road here was originally intended to have verges, cycle lanes and surface junctions – just as the current vogue is for boulevards and shared use – rather than the grade separation that town planner Colin Buchanan eventually advocated in the 1960s.

The later modernism of the eastern side of Coventry's city centre, beyond Basil Spence's cathedral, is altogether tougher and more space-age. Roads literally penetrate buildings and no fewer than three different structures fly over streets in short order, including the brutalist Britannia hotel by G.R. Stone and the infamous 1976 Elephant leisure centre.

Here, the ring road stomps gruffly above the city on concrete stilts. 'It seemed to represent some things that were subcultural,' says Steiner. At its heart, Disappear Here is set on reframing the perception of a ring road as a piece of prosaic infrastructure associated with traffic, segregation and crime. 'We wanted to capture a little bit of the spirit of that older Coventry too,' he adds. 'This environment is strange and alien, yet familiar.'

'The ring road somewhat restricts the city, it doesn't allow anything out,' says film-maker Emilia Moniszko, who moved to Coventry from Poland and collaborated with Bridgewater on one of the poetry films.

'The road is a ring – but it's a forced marriage,' echoes Antony Owen, another of the poets involved in the project.

Alice in Covland, a film by Leanne Bridgewater and Moniszko, mixes *Donnie Darko* gloom with people dancing on overpasses and running through subways to Bridgewater's refrain, 'I'm late, I'm late – for a very important date.'

'Concrete structures convey quite a romantic ideology,' says Moniszko. 'We're trying to demonstrate this with a rabbit who's lost in Coventry. He keeps trying to find himself, trying to find potential and purpose.' At one point the rabbit amusingly checks out hoardings advertising a rising residential development near the road.

'The rabbit can run all it wants,' Bridgewater adds, 'but the road is a circle so we just go round and round.'

Getting lost crops up a lot in the poems, as do subways. Poet Richard Houguez and film-maker Dora Mortimer's piece lingers on the neon lighting you find in such underpasses. Film-maker Ben Cook and poet Sarah James compared the whooshing car headlights along the ring road to the River Sherbourne which runs under the city and cuts across the road, but which the council is planning to open up in the future.

Motorways and ring roads aren't the most obvious subject for poets – though Simon Armitage was inspired by the M62 and Lorna Dee Cervantes by California's Freeway 280. 'It's a hard sell to get people interested in what's in front of them – this concrete superstructure,' says Steiner. 'But the poets have reimagined and re-presented what's under our noses. It's part of the sense maybe of renewed optimism in the city right now.'

Armitage's poem, 'Horses, M62', talks of a nag on the hard shoulder: 'It bolts, all arse and tail through a valley of fleet saloons.' Cervantes paints a vivid picture of the eponymous northern Californian artery and the life underneath it: 'But under the fake windsounds of the open lanes, in the abandoned lots below, new grasses sprout, wild mustard remembers, old gardens come back stronger than they were.'

Brave flaneurs find unusual enjoyment in these apparently oppressive spaces. The Specials found inspiration here, and in Steven Knight's 2024 bravura BBC drama *This Town*, set in early 1980s 'Cov' and 'Brum', our hero Dante Brown returns to the same bridge above the motorway to compose his poetry and lyrics.

'I enjoy standing underneath the ring road, listening to the cars,' Bridgewater reflects. 'This is Coventry's version of listening to the sea.'

Crowds at the Super Prix

Super Prix course, Birmingham

ROAD RACING
IN BIRMINGHAM

With its majestic motorways twisting and turning around town, sprawling ring roads, crazy car parks on steroids, and a healthy devotion to vehicle making and motorsport, Birmingham is the UK's undisputed car capital. It had the first one-way streets, the first houses with built-in garages, and the National Exhibition Centre was for many years the home of the British International Motor Show.

Jonathan Meades made a furiously funny BBC TV film about the roads of 'Brum' called *Heart By-Pass*, while writer Jonathan Coe set his novel *The Rotters' Club* around a car factory his dad worked in (the city was the centre of the British motor manufacturing industry – the home of Rover, Austin, MG, Jaguar, Land Rover and Lucas).

But Brum really pushed the boat out by building miles of motorways in the 1960s and 70s, from the famous Spaghetti Junction all the way into the city centre itself. The result was a surreal supercharged landscape. These superfast, superwide roads became the perfect place to host legal street races (though Brummies have always had a penchant for the illegal kind too – out near the Star City leisure park you can find young men racing their cars around at night).

Starting in 1986, Birmingham became the Monte Carlo of the Midlands and closed a huge chunk of roads down to host a massive motor-race. Petrolheads revel in the memories of those hot summer 80s days which were soundtracked by Birmingham band Duran Duran. They're also trying to resurrect the race – which ran for 4km down Bristol Road, Belgrave Middleway and through Digbeth – for a new generation. But why?

'My dad is a huge motorsport fan. My younger sister started racing Ministox and my dad would tell us about the Superprix every time we'd go racing at Birmingham Wheels or eat a curry on Ladypool Road – just off the Superprix course,' remembers Andy Smallman, a film-maker born in Birmingham in the year the final race was held, 1990.

'It always fascinated me – and this was pre-Internet days when I could only use my imagination. Years later I found a book on the subject, and as soon as I opened it I couldn't believe the scale of the whole Superprix thing, but also how little the city had documented it. I immediately went home and searched for more information, and when I watched race footage it just reinforced my fascination. Now I could put it into context: watching them race down roads I know so well yet could never imagine future F1 world champions had stormed down in their Formula 3000 cars.' Those future stars included Damon Hill, Jean Alesi and Mika Häkkinen.

Now Smallman and his dedicated band of fellow car enthusiasts are documenting the history of the races – and will eventually release a feature-length film documenting the tale of this high-octane slice of Birmingham's automotive history.

'The project is multi-media based and the film is just one part of that. We collect interviews and memories from racing drivers, marshals, officials and the fans. The other side is our archive, where we collect physical and digital pieces of memorabilia, information, footage and photos so that we can preserve and build a detailed timeline and history of the Superprix for future generations,' explains Smallman.

Smallman has worked with fellow Brummies to put out Superprix-branded T-shirts, and even a craft beer. 'We collaborated with other local independent businesses like Two Towers Brewery, Provide and Space. Play on unique products such as clothing, craft design and beverages. We have also held events and brought all of our resources together for occasions to celebrate the Birmingham Superprix, like the Autosport International show at the NEC.'

As if all this history wasn't intriguing enough, the next chapter could be the best of all. Because Birmingham has recently realized the power of the Superprix – and wants to bring the smell of petrol and the blistering noise of racing-car engines back to the city's streets. And the support goes to the very top.

The intense competition for F1 races probably precludes a full F1 Grand Prix in the mould of the Monaco, Valencia or Singapore street circuits. But

Super Prix racing

perhaps the small but growing Formula E electric-car series might come to Brum?

'Formula E is a possibility,' agrees Andy Smallman. 'I believe we stand a strong chance to look into this as a realistic venture to chase. The original race was pushed through with immense speed and urgency, going from Parliament to reality within just a few years. If this became a reality again, I'd love to think at least some parts of the original track would remain in the new course — just to pay tribute to its history. But that would depend on modern-day safety regulations and track logistics.'

THE CAR PARK
IS BEING REINVENTED

The car park is being reinvented. And, perhaps surprisingly, art is at the forefront. We are turning multi-storeys into galleries, parachuting hipster sculpture parks onto car-park roofs, flipping parking spaces into cool living spaces, and reappraising parking architecture.

The unassuming Hurst Street car park in Birmingham hosted the city's Ikon Gallery and Hippodrome theatre's About Town festival of video art — showing Gillian Wearing's 'Broad Street', which depicts tipsy clubbers in 2001 on the city's main nightlife drag, and Oliver Beer's 'Pay and Display' — a collaboration with the Ex Cathedra choir, incredibly inspired by the eerie echo of a stairwell in a nearby Brum car park.

'The brutalist car park where I made "Pay and Display" is matter-of-fact, prosaic architecture — but its acoustics are as pure and beautiful as those of any cathedral,' Beer says. 'The building will be wiped out in the next phase of development, and for me the sound piece I made there was almost an aural cast of the architecture.'

These days, we take the train or the bus when we can. So many city car parks lie half-empty. 'While changing lifestyles mean that there is less demand for parking, the public's interest in art is greater than ever,' says Sean Bidder of The Vinyl Factory, who set up a gallery inside Brewer Street car park in Soho — hosting work by Quentin Jones and Robert Storey. For fellow

Welbeck St Car Park

Bold Tendencies, London, UK

artist Lorenzo Belenguer, the car park beneath Cavendish Square in central London – where he exhibited as part of the Frieze Festival fringe – worked because 'its minimalist design makes it exceptionally suited for contemporary art'.

Since 2007, the Bold Tendencies group has transformed Peckham's multi-storey into an annual outdoor gallery, topped by the trendy Frank's Café. Now, small towns are joining in: Ruthin's new Art Trail turned the boring height barriers on car parks in the North Wales town into sculpture – embedding them with retro photos or vintage train tickets.

In the US, they're experimenting with living in car parks. Students at the Savannah College of Art and Design (Scad) in Georgia designed prototype digs – Scadpads. Cheap, colourful, parking-space-sized and perched high in Atlanta and Savannah multi-storeys – perfect, if you don't have much stuff. 'Parking structures haven't been examined as opportunities for urban living,' believes Christian Sottile, the former dean of Scad's School of Building Arts. 'We see these 20th-century structures as a huge opportunity to bring art and design together and sustainably evolve these buildings.'

But can car parks be works of art in themselves? Miami thinks so. It has commissioned garages from famous architects, such as the elegant 'urban experience' at 1111 Lincoln Road, by the Swiss firm Herzog & de Meuron. Or Sheffield's attention-seeking Charles Street car park by architects Allies and Morrison, which looks like a series of half-completed Rubik's cubes, and won a RIBA Award in 2009.

Even our maligned 1970s car parks can seem beautiful. Hove's Norton Road car park and Birmingham's Moat Lane and Newhall Street multi-storeys had a certain tough aesthetic to them. Illustrator Stephen Millership was beguiled by the sinuous car-park decks on top of Preston's bus station, reproducing them recently as a poster in his kitsch 'Lost Destinations' series. The Welbeck Street car park in London's West End was beloved by many for its kooky façade and a lot of people were sad to see it go in the name of modernization.

The Royal Society of Arts called for empty British car parks to be turned into drive-in cinemas, skating rinks or tennis courts. As our car parks increasingly lie empty, it seems ever more tempting to turn them into something more fun, swapping pay and display for play and display.

DeLorean car

THE DELOREAN STORY

The peace line – one of the metal-and-concrete barriers separating Belfast's nationalist and unionist neighbourhoods – disappears into the foggy distance, and I ask Ken, my affable taxi driver, if he thinks they'll ever be got rid of.

His almost comically aggressive 'No!' is like a ton of bricks coming down around my inquiry. He's that sick of tourists asking the same thing. I look out through the car window, puzzling at the murals and messages emblazoned on the barrier, and we move on. Belfast has a fraught relationship with roads and cars.

You can take these taxi tours out to the Falls Road and the Shankill Road, but the peace lines make it impossible to keep your bearings.

Blocking roads has always been a political act here. During the Troubles, Republicans and Loyalists did it with makeshift barricades to protect their areas, and the British Army did it with their own fortifications.

Car bombs were a way of life, as well as death, and certain vehicles acquired a distinctiveness. The IRA drove Austin Marinas and Ford Escorts. When British soldiers took to the road, they did so in pug-nosed Saracen armoured personnel carriers and Land Rovers.

But in the midst of the Troubles it was a different kind of vehicle entirely that came to define Northern Ireland. It was neither a drab British marque nor a piece of alienating military hardware. Instead, it was something exotic, futuristic, fantastical and glamorous, speaking of a world a million miles from a province plunged into darkness by brutal sectarian violence. It was the DeLorean DMC-12 – a revolutionary US sports car. Decades on from Ulster becoming the unlikeliest location for what would prove to be short-lived DeLorean production, the car is firing people's imaginations all over again.

The creation of swaggering American auto icon John Zachary DeLorean, its unique styling by the Piedmontese design maestro Giorgetto Giugiaro, the DeLorean is one of the most recognizable cars ever made. Even people who are car-clueless know a DeLorean when those gull-wing doors pop open; when they eye that distinctive boxy profile.

I became fascinated by the DeLorean some years ago and soon discovered that I was not alone. (A recent documentary, Netflix's 2021 *Myth & Mogul*, delves into John's colourful life.) But which soil did the dream emerge from? DeLorean built his factory in the Dunmurry area of Belfast, which stood – symbolically enough – on a bog between the Protestant Lisburn Road and the Catholic Twinbrook estate. Twinbrook was the home of hunger striker Bobby Sands, who worked in the motor industry himself before he died in Long Kesh prison as the first DMC-12s arrived.

John DeLorean was from a city less cramped but no less segregated than Belfast. Detroit is wide open. You can (if you've got the legs for it) stroll through deserted plots, between community allotments and strip clubs, strip malls and dive bars. There's segregation, but it's more subtle – there aren't fences and walls like in Belfast – there are freeways and spaces, sky and emptiness. Right in Detroit's bullseye is the gaudy, post-modern HQ of General Motors, the corporation that John DeLorean rose through the ranks of as a charismatic executive. He loved to party with Hollywood producers, TV stars and models. He was a celebrity with the gift of the gab. And when he persuaded the British Labour government in 46 days flat to stump up subsidies for his factory in Dunmurry, he finally got what he wanted: the chance to make his own car. The diggers moved in to start construction of the plant in October 1978, as The Undertones' 'Teenage Kicks' came out. Suddenly, not everything in Ulster came back to bombs.

These were strange times. The dominance of the American car industry, and of the fast-talkers who ran it and sold its products, is reminiscent of *Mad Men*. I'm reminded of Don's escapes in his car; Joan's horrifying night with the Jaguar dealer. As a character, DeLorean was as mysterious as any of the fictional rogues of Madison Avenue, but in Ulster in the late 1970s he inspired devotion.

By 1982, however, the company was in a hole. A perfect storm had taken its toll: poor sales, recession, a bleak American winter, lukewarm reviews — especially of the car's under-powered engine. DeLorean and Margaret Thatcher's Tory government seemed at war. The plant needed cash. It wasn't forthcoming and eventually everyone was laid off. The dream had died. In October 1982 the FBI carried out a sting operation on DeLorean, and the resulting video appeared to show him toasting a forthcoming drug deal. Did he take the bait because he wanted to save DMC? Or was it a set-up? DeLorean was acquitted of all charges two years later. But in Britain the whiff of impropriety wouldn't go away. Money had vanished. DeLorean never returned for questioning.

Barrie Wills worked as DMC director of purchasing, director of supplies, director of product development. I ask him whether he thought DeLorean's rags to riches to rags story is similar to the car's? Wills, who ended up in 1982 with what he called 'the somewhat dubious title of acting chief executive in receivership', replies: 'Very similar. But I would prefer to focus on the positives which Northern Ireland should celebrate and maybe even use as a tourist attraction, alongside the *Titanic* — as an example of the technical and operational achievements of Northern Irish workers.'

The truth is that the DeLorean renaissance is already under way. It's inspiring films, music, books and art. The car still matters to people — especially in its home, Ulster.

Of course, that's in part due to the enduring popularity of *Back to the Future*, which featured the DeLorean as a time machine. *Back to the Future Part II* imagined the world in 2015 — DeLoreans were still a part of it. In fact this stainless-steel car is as popular as ever. Of the 9,080 built at Dunmurry, 6,500 remain worldwide.

It's not just Robert Zemeckis and Steven Spielberg who were influenced by DeLorean's car. Basque band DeLorean chose a name befitting their retro-futurist Balearic sound. And in 2008, the musician Gruff Rhys released a highly polished concept album about John DeLorean, called *Stainless Style*. When I reviewed it for the music website Drowned in Sound, I knew nothing about DeLorean's life — but since that point he, and his car, have got under my skin.

Other people have felt it, too. 'Much of my work is based on chasing up rumours and lost histories,' explains artist Sean Lynch. 'I took a particular interest in DeLorean — my father ran a garage in Ireland for 25 years. I heard a rumour about the leftovers of the factory ending up at the bottom of the Atlantic Ocean and so began a search through the scrapyards of Ireland to try and verify this story.'

Lynch's wanderlust ended up with an exhibition called DeLorean: Progress Report, which impressed London's art crowds. Lynch found the remains of the cars that had been dumped in the sea off Ireland and photographed them with lobsters poking out from their submerged chassis. Another artist, Cyril Hatt, also created a piece of DeLorean art. Along with 150 ex-employees, Hatt built a sculpture of a DMC-12 made from photographs stuck on metal. Many of those DMC line workers – and their colleagues from Lotus who also worked on it – gathered in Belfast in 2015 for a reunion.

Barrie Wills, who wrote a memoir called *John Z, the DeLorean and Me*, helped to organize it: 'The reunion was the first ever. It celebrated the anniversary of the first public showing in the spring of 1980 of the "Visioneering" [prototype] car, manufactured as a joint exercise by DeLorean, Lotus and Visioneering personnel in Fraser, near Detroit.'

It wasn't just workers who gathered in Belfast, it was fans of the car, too.

'I saw them on TV back in the 1970s. I thought, "That's a damn good idea!"', remembers Dave Howarth, owner of three DMC-12s and President of the British DeLorean Owners Club. 'I was a plumbing and heating engineer back then and my hands were ripped to pieces with stainless steel. Well, maybe a car made of it was for me.'

Things got serious for Howarth. 'I went to the Motor Show in 1981 and thought, "I'm gonna have one of these." It cost £16,283 – twice the price of a Porsche! To me, they still look as modern as they did then.' Howarth's cars had some famous owners. 'One, John Taylor of Duran Duran owned. One of the others was owned by DeLorean's brother-in-law.' I ask Howarth whether he thinks that DeLorean was guilty of fraud, of conspiracy to supply drugs. 'No! He did what he said he would do.' Howarth is convinced that John was only trying to save the plant.

Many of the car's most ardent fans, and some ex-employees, forgive John's sins. They see him as someone who wanted to create something unique, who supplied jobs to Northern Ireland when it needed them most, and who fought against the cartel of American auto makers.

Did the big companies have it in for John? In an eye-opening ATV documentary from 1981 directed by D.A. Pennebaker, John DeLorean is filmed telling a New Orleans talk-radio host that it would take a big car company 'seven or eight seconds' to finish him off – if they wanted to. John laughs. But was he joking?

John DeLorean

INTERVIEWS

Lisa Brown

@LISAINLEEDS / PHOTOGRAPHER AND MAKER

Tell us about your experiences of carchitecture, Lisa — we've talked about Keighley's rebuilt town centre and of course the Arndale in Bradford where my granny worked and which you know so well!

My favourite building in Keighley is the car park at the Airedale Centre — although ironically I have never been into it in a car! It's covered in these amazing twisted fin-shaped panels — which are really striking and stand out among all the Victorian Yorkshire stone buildings in the town.

I think my most memorable carchitecture structures are motorway services. They were like landmarks marking your way to or from somewhere, and if they had a Little Chef or a Happy Eater, then there was also the allure of the exciting roadside restaurant.

My other iconic structures were the cooling towers near Sheffield and an old windmill which we passed on the way to Blackpool to see the illuminations; a marker that meant we were almost there.

I was thinking about some of the quirkier by-products of the car in Yorkshire, like drive-thru fish-and-chip super-shops like Harry Ramsden's etc. How did these come about and do you have any memories of them?

I actually can't remember going to any of the drive-thru chip shops. My dad did sometimes go

Airedale Centre, Keighley

out of his way to get chips — but that was because the tiny one in our village was barely ever open!

I think Harry Ramsden's prided itself on being incredibly modern — but obviously incredibly traditional at the same time!

Thinking about other countries, any kinds of car-led modernism that has taken your eye, like malls, supermarkets, car parks, services and civil engineering?

I am slightly obsessed by the shaped structures you get in the US; oranges, bottles, shoes and a teapot are all examples I have seen. I did make a special trip to the Donut Hole in La Puente in LA, because of course I want to drive through a doughnut and buy a doughnut! They have just the right amount of kitsch, but are of course incredibly practical for such a car-centric country as they really stand out as you whizz by.

There is a great example of something similar in Wales — a kiosk shaped like an apple. Amazing!

Wondering how — as a fan of modernism but also caring about the environment, like me — you see ways that we can be more green and make cities more liveable but keep these important symbols of the 20th century alive?

I think that's exactly it — we need to keep them. It should always be a last resort to demolish.

We need to be so much more imaginative than we are at the moment, and if it was harder to knock something down it would force that creativity into being.

Orange World,
Florida, USA

Felix Torkar

ON BRUTALISM AND ROADS INTERSECTING

SOSBRUTALISM.ORG

Felix, you are 'one of the people' behind SOS Brutalism, which I very much enjoyed contributing to. Are there special examples of car-related brutalism around the world you like?

Paul Rudolph's Temple Street parking garage in New Haven (1963) is an early favourite. When I finally visited it a few years back, I was gobsmacked by just how big of a difference the ultra-raw cast-in-place concrete really makes in person compared to the usual prefab fare. Beyond that, I am particularly fond of more outlandish projects. For the Arlington Temple (Arlington, VA, 1971) architect Vlastimil Koubek was briefed with the challenge to design a church on top of a gas station on an inclined, triangle-shaped lot and it's glorious! Sadly now demolished is the Mercedes-Benz dealership Automóviles Louzao in Coruña, Spain, with a particularly adventurous dangling glass showroom. Lastly, J.Mayer.H's highway gas station in Georgia from 2011 is a great example of the resurgence of brutalist principles in recent years.

And in Germany what carchitecture on or near roads do you think is worth seeking out? Any cool engineering or buildings?

Lothar Götz's mesmerizing BP Tankstellenpavillon Fulda (1952) looked like a hovering, glowing UFO at night. It strikes me as an early precursor to the Steve Jobs Theater.

Hanielgarage, Dusseldorf

The Hanielgarage by Paul Schneider-Esleben is from 1953, but still looks contemporary today. The parking garage plus motel concept might seem a little outdated, but the beautiful suspended ramp is still a feat of engineering. Conceptually similarly outdated but particularly curious is Berlin's Parking Garage and Apartment Complex Kirchbachstraße 1 & 2 (Peter Heinrichs / Joachim Wermund, 1979). A giant robot in a small residential street!

We are both very fond of this era but obviously a lot of concrete was used and a lot of top-down planning was enacted. Can we preserve these icons while also addressing climate problems and planning for the future somehow?

Not only *can* we preserve these icons, we must! It is critical in our collective response to climate change and resource scarcity to stop continuously demolishing and rebuilding. We have the opportunity to preserve this enormous amount of resources that went into these projects half a century ago. If we can find concepts that allow us to continue to use or reuse those structures, we can greatly reduce the necessity to spend even more resources for new construction projects today. Therefore, heritage conservation should be considered an indispensable pillar for a sustainable future.

Apartment Complex
Kirchbachstraße
1 & 2, Berlin

Mary Keating

AUTHOR OF *BIRMINGHAM: THE BRUTIFUL YEARS*

@BRUTIFULBIRMINGHAM

Tell us about the story of the Ringway Centre and Smallbrook Queensway and why you want to save it.

When I was a little girl we came into Birmingham city centre for shopping and special occasions. The bus travelled down the Hagley Road and there were certain landmarks I was excited to check off as we approached our goal. The concrete cats on the roof of a large Edwardian villa. The little round modern building outside the AA offices. Five Ways Island and the wonderful coloured-glass frieze that cascaded down the side of Auchinleck House – a 1950s modernist office block. But I knew we had really arrived when the bus travelled alongside the magnificent sweep of the Ringway Centre running down Smallbrook

Queensway with its modern, abstract concrete relief and the glamorous uplighters. For anyone who wants a taste of that excitement and what it is like to drive past this building, just look at the Harold Baim film of Birmingham in the late 70s/early 80s: *Telly Savalas Looks at Birmingham*.

What about Birmingham today?

Travelling into Birmingham now, all of these landmarks are gone. The final axe fell on the Ringway Centre on 28 September 2023 when the planning committee narrowly approved total demolition. In 2024 an application to the High Court for a judicial review was unsuccessful. The Ringway Centre was designed by James

Smallbrook
Queensway,
Birmingham, UK

Roberts — he of Birmingham Rotunda fame. Roberts was a son of Birmingham: he was born here, trained here and practised as an architect here. I particularly like this human story of how he conceived the development of the Queensway. He did not see active service in the war due to a disability but was a fire-watcher, his post being on top of the Council House. In the many hours he spent in this eyrie he decided that what Birmingham needed was a watchtower. The idea for the Rotunda was born. The construction of the first part of the new inner ring road, Smallbrook Queensway, left a narrow strip of land running down one side of the road. Roberts was good at fitting things into awkward spaces. His vision of the Gated City Wall with the watchtower at one end and his two high-rise blocks, the Sentinels, framing the gateway at the other end was complete.

What's unique about the Ringway Centre?

At 228m (750ft) long, the Ringway Centre was, when it was constructed, one of the longest shop frontages in the country. The repetition of the concrete relief is meant to be seen from a car. Gliding past, it allows a chance to acknowledge the building and at the same time gives the passenger an entertaining journey. The building has been twice recommended for statutory listing — on the first occasion the criticism included comment that it was too repetitive! I am not the only one wanting to save this iconic Birmingham building and indeed the support for its preservation is considerable, from the Twentieth Century Society to Extinction Rebellion to members of Birmingham's LGBTQ+ community (Birmingham's LGBTQ+ quarter begins under the building and runs down Hurst Street). Our campaign group brought together a diverse group to pool our talents: Brutiful Birmingham, Zero Carbon House, Birmingham Modernists and C20 Society. There is no longer one argument for its redemption. Its unique Birmingham heritage value — epitomizing Birmingham, 'the City of the Car' — is an important consideration but the climate emergency is an equal if not greater concern. We should not demolish these buildings.

Rotunda,
Birmingham, UK

Chris Marshall

ON BRITAIN'S MOST INTERESTING ROAD ENGINEERING

RUNS ROADS.ORG.UK

What examples of car-centric architecture around the world do you like — buildings by the roadside, anything quirky especially?

I have a real soft spot for service areas that have the restaurant on a bridge over the motorway. Leicester Forest East is the one I always think of, probably because I went there a number of times as a small child and found it oddly thrilling to sit at a table, eating lunch while the traffic rushed underneath you. There are only a few of them around, but they are wonderfully telling about the era in which they were built: imagine thinking the motorway was so novel, and so fascinating, that people would want to look at it while they were having a break from driving on it.

Forton Services, UK

The other service-area building I really love is the Pennine Tower at Forton Services. It long ago fell into disuse, because it's patently impractical, but it has the most wonderful *Thunderbirds* appearance and it's an unmissable landmark as you go past on the M6. It comes from that same period of genuine excitement and enthusiasm for the rapidly expanding motorway network, and it was built to give you a view of the road, but it was also designed to lift travellers up above the trees and show them the place they were passing through. From the restaurant deck or the glass-screened roof terrace (yes, really) you get the most unexpectedly panoramic view: you can see the Lake District, Blackpool Tower, the Forest of Bowland and the distant Pennines. What an astonishing thing to build.

One other that fascinates me in France, but where there's not actually much to see, is the Triangle de Rocquencourt near Paris – it's a triangular motorway interchange laid out in the late 1930s, but only completed in about 1950 (for obvious reasons). It was designed to incorporate a lighthouse-like monument in the middle, called the Signal of the Three Provinces, marking the confluence of roads from Normandy, Brittany and the Ile-de-France; by the time it was finished, though, that sort of hubris had left the French motorway programme and all that was built was the platform it would have stood on. But you can still get there, apparently, along an overgrown path, an underpass and a grand staircase, to stand on a classical plinth in the middle of a motorway junction where all the flyovers have ornate balustrades. A google image search for '*signal des trois-provinces rocquencourt*' turns up some nice artist's impressions of what might have been a striking monument to the motor age.

Which are your favourite examples in Leeds and the north of England?

In the 1930s Leeds built a new east–west street through the city centre, variously named Westgate, Eastgate and the Headrow – it was very much intended to be a grand thoroughfare, almost like

Leicester Forest East
Services, UK

Triangle de
Rocquencort, France

a ceremonial or processional avenue, lined with grand new buildings, intended to help the city get to grips with motor traffic. At its eastern end it meets Kirkgate and Regent Street at a roundabout, which — as originally built — contained a petrol station in the middle. It survived long enough that I remember seeing it, and even visiting it once or twice, when I was driven around Leeds as a child in the late 80s and early 90s.

The petrol station and its kiosk building was a dilapidated thing by then, and horribly dangerous to get in and out of. It closed in about 1995 and now the building has been repurposed as a sort of greenhouse full of tropical plants to make a centrepiece for the junction. The building itself is a stylish hexagonal pavilion with a peaked roof, and was clearly designed to be a focal point. Around it you can still see the forecourt and its three openings onto the roundabout. It's a lovely bit of urban design, forming a full stop at the end of the long hill down Eastgate, balancing the open space of the junction with the tall buildings around it, and making clever use of otherwise dead space in the days when traffic was light enough to make it viable. You couldn't really use it for anything now, so it is just ornamental, but it's very much architecture that exists solely because of the motor car, and completely in service of it.

Which roads do you think were particularly well executed and which pieces of civil engineering on and around them do you think are good?

I've always thought the Leeds Inner Ring Road is a great piece of design, and not just from a sense of hometown pride. In the sixties there were a number of inner-city motorways built in the UK; their designers thought they'd be the first of many, but changes in policy around motoring in towns, and an unexpectedly strong public backlash against urban motorways, meant we didn't get many more after that.

Most of those 60s urban motorways are now considered an ugly inconvenience or are actively hated. The Westway might be the most famous, and despite all the redevelopment that surrounds it, it's still a visible and noisy scar through west London. In Birmingham, the council has spent the last 20 years trying to dismantle the Inner Ring Road, which they memorably described as 'choking' the city. Manchester, Glasgow and Newcastle have love-hate relationships with their central motorways. But in Leeds, the same doesn't seem to apply. Nobody seems to mind the Inner Ring Road, and I think that's because of its design.

Unlike all the others it goes out of its way to hide from view — there are tunnel sections, and most of the parts in the open air are sunken into deep trenches so you can't see it, and don't really hear it, until you cross it on a bridge and suddenly realize it's there. That means it doesn't scar the urban landscape in the same way and doesn't form such an unwelcome imposition. And the service it performs is obvious — the city centre in Leeds is increasingly pedestrianized, and the degree to which it is car-free and walkable is in no small part thanks to the Inner Ring Road pushing traffic out of the way and underground. It is probably the UK's most thoughtfully designed and least obtrusive urban motorway, and the greatest credit you can pay its designers is that, unlike all of its peers, nobody seems to really notice it's there.

Why are the Leeds Inner Ring Road junctions so bonkers?

I suppose because it's trying to do a lot in a small space. There are many junctions placed close together so the designers used all sorts of tricks — braiding, parallel carriageways and in one place an off-side exit — to allow sliproads from adjoining junctions to overlap without crowding the main carriageways. It's very clever design but feels very unorthodox today.

Dr Dawn Pereira

ON PUBLIC ART IN THE AGE OF CARS

AUTHOR OF *THE COLOURFUL CRUSADE OF WILLIAM MITCHELL: THE INTEGRATION OF ARCHITECTURAL SCULPTURE INTO POST-WAR URBAN LANDSCAPES (1957-77)*

Tell us about William Mitchell's unique roundabout sculptures at Hockley Circus in Birmingham.

The *Birmingham Post*'s headline from March 1968 described William Mitchell's series of cast concrete murals at Hockley Circus as 'the oddest – and toughest' and explained they were intended to contrast with the 'rigidity and precision of the environment created by the viaduct and subways'. An article in the *Concrete* journal revealed that the actual design of the murals was unknown before the arrival of the polystyrene liners, but the contractor's R.M. Douglas Construction Limited had considered that the placing of the concrete in the 'delicate and intricate moulds' had been a difficult task but 'carried out most successfully'.

William Mitchell's ambitious contribution at Hockley Circus was designed for the pedestrian rather than the car user, who may only have just caught a glimpse of the concrete relief surfaces as they zoomed past on the roundabout or from the flyover above. The sunken concourse was initially designed with a paved area, public conveniences and three glass kiosks, with the largest structure planned as a café. To 'add a touch of softness' to the landscaped areas, children from the nearby Hockley junior and infant schools had been invited to plant twelve rowan trees. Among all this activity, children were often photographed in imaginative play or found dangling from the deep relief surfaces.

Described by the *Birmingham Post* as 'abstracts of concrete', the 'white' mural contained an

William Mitchell at work

216

over-arching triangular shape impressed with rhythmic patterns of signature doughnuts and geometric shapes. From afar the eye is drawn to a giant sunburst and convex moonscape features, yet when close to, hands are enticed into the voids filled with teeth-like dentils. The more 'greyish' mural cast in 'ordinary Portland' cement possesses a series of vertical ribs protruding at different depths, the rugged stepped textures inviting the adventurous to climb; for the more curious-minded, individual bold motifs are tucked away on the sides that mount the grassy slopes. The sculptural 'terracotta' wall possesses giant triangular wedges and circle motifs faceted at conflicting angles, creating imagery from a strange face profile to practically flying kinetic motifs but contrasted by sections of ancient rune-like language, drawing the viewer to calmly ponder their meaning.

How and why did they get commissioned and is there anything else like them?

By the mid-1960s, William Mitchell became known locally in Birmingham through a set of 19 cast concrete relief sandblasted panels positioned above the ground floor level of Broadgate House (Rail House), a 15-storey office and showroom complex designed by architect John Madin on Broad Street in 1965. In May 1967, Mitchell illustrated his versatility further, exhibiting

Mitchell's Hockley sculptures, Birmingham, UK

'The Magi' sculptures at the Building Centre in Broad Street, with the three 2.75m-high (9ft) figures carved from thermalite using a spontaneous grit-blasting technique. The Hockley Circus reliefs were commissioned by Birmingham Corporation's Public Works Department in conjunction with architect James A. Roberts, who designed the concourse elements, and R.E. Slater, who designed the flyover. The flyover was opened on 1 April 1968 by Sir Bertram Waring, chairman of Joseph Lucas Ltd, and cost £2,500,000, with work having started in September 1965.

William Mitchell considered that one had to be a salesman to get through committee meetings and, while sharing how he planned to 'enliven' Birmingham to a town hall full of people, realized that 'they were out to get him'. He didn't mind; it was all 'part of the process'. By March 1968, the *Birmingham Post* revealed that three design teams had been asked by the Birmingham Corporation to submit proposals for Hockley's pedestrian concourse, with William Mitchell Design Consultants chosen for a fee of £4,750.

These artworks remain unique in his oeuvre and capture the qualities that were essential to a successful Mitchell commission: affordable and resistant to vandalism, part of a major construction job and accessible but intriguing enough for the public to perpetually enjoy.

Maybe tell us a little about the Horsefair and JFK mosaics, but also the incredible Kenneth Budd.

The origin of Kenneth Budd's commissions in Birmingham came through the first murals he created for Colmore Circus, as part of the Queensway Inner Ring Road. Initially William Mitchell and Associates had been commissioned by the Public Works Department to create two 15x3.6m (50x12ft) mosaic murals, at a cost of £2,000 each. However, as Budd had worked as one of Mitchell's 'associates' from 1961–65 and Mitchell was inundated with work, Budd had been invited by the artist to fulfil these commissions.

Kenneth Budd's son Oliver, in his book *Budd Mosaics*, revealed that his dad worked through many sketches and ideas when planning a design to show a client, and his visualization was often in the form of a painted picture. Based on historical research Budd had undertaken at Birmingham's Central Library, the first Colmore mural, which faced the Gaumont Cinema, reached fruition in 1964 and depicted a battle scene between Royalist and Parliamentary forces during the English Civil War. The second, completed in 1965, by the Colmore Precinct, illustrated Birmingham at the time of the Industrial Revolution. Budd's small-scale drawing transposed into a full-scale paper cartoon, which was then skilfully depicted in broken ceramic

JFK Mosaic,
Birmingham, UK

tiles attached to expanded aluminium mesh panels and grouted on site.

When planning for the urban landscape, Kenneth Budd told the *Municipal Journal* in 1966 that he considered the pedestrian as a 'creature of habit', hardly noticing the path taken daily for a lifetime, so that it came as a rude shock when that path vanished, and their familiar route was replaced by a confusing maze of steps, ramps and underpasses. He felt the answer was to examine every detail of the public experience, with all amenities 'carefully chosen to be in satisfying relation with each other'.

Through his initial experience of working with Mitchell and then freelance, Budd gained the necessary technical skills, knowledge and confidence to secure more prestigious commissions and develop these in his own style, with Birmingham's profusion of underpasses providing ideal backdrops. One of his most well-known and popular outcomes was his powerful smalti mosaic 'Kennedy Memorial' designed for the Irish Catholic Committee, which was unveiled in 1969.

Are there any other examples of William Mitchell works related to cars and roads or the automobile age in general? He did some work in malls like the Bradford Arndale, didn't he, but tell us about anything else?

With roads providing a framework for towns and cities, and the car increasingly shaping the landscape, William Mitchell's first commissions relating to transport infrastructure were a series of mixed-media and concrete murals situated in the heart of London within the pedestrian subways of the 'Marble Arch – Hyde Park Corner' road improvement scheme (1962) created for the London County Council as part of their Patronage of the Arts scheme. He also contributed a concrete sampler frieze that ran the full length of a revolutionary carpark containing car elevator platforms, at Emanuel House in Rochester Row (1968).

In Birmingham, Mitchell had already created sculptural concrete panels for the exterior of Rail House and was accredited with the Colmore Circus 'Civil War' and 'Industrial Revolution' murals, although sub-contracted to associate Kenneth Budd. His glass-fibre frieze at Lucas Industries Technical Centre near Solihull (1965) hinted at all kinds of engineering and technological parts and instruments, related to their work on the fuel and electronic systems for the supersonic Concorde airliner, with their equipment also found in the Rolls-Royce RB211 and the advanced passenger liner, *Queen Elizabeth II*.

These commissions would lead to the more complex structural infrastructure project at the Hockley Flyover, which contained deeply sculptured patterned walls at the entrance of the three subways for children to climb on. Mitchell was heavily involved with the industrial and engineering side of concrete through his lectures for the Cement & Concrete Association in Britain and internationally, but also through creating display works for their headquarters at Wexham Springs. This led to more practical applications, devising heavily textured in-situ retaining walls cast from glass-fibre mould liners that could be reused extensively. Mitchell represented the artistic potential of concrete on many advisory boards, including those related to formwork, and this input coincided with the development of cutting-edge civil engineering and landscaping developments for motorways.

Mitchell's first pivotal collaboration was with pioneer engineers Ove Arup & Partners (under Povl Ahm) and architects Sir Basil Spence, Bonnington & Collins, at Gateshead Viaduct (1971), to create a series of glass-fibre moulds that could be grouped together to make a shutter lining that would be craned into place and made good by the construction workers as part of the formwork. This

Close-up of JFK Mosaic, UK

same pattern was subsequently found in different configurations at the south end of the Cuilfail Tunnel (1975) in Lewes and on retaining walls of what would become the M25 near Reigate (1976). He then moved on to the Middlesbrough Bypass (1975), working with chief engineer Bill Douglas to specifically develop a design that minimized the potential for water staining or streaking.

Technical concrete publications began to feature appealing images of William Mitchell's exposed concrete finishes, capturing further experiments to tackle weathering and enhance kinetic qualities for drivers, with his contribution particularly visible in Michael Gage's detailed technical book *Guide to Exposed Concrete Finishes* (1970). These developments led to one of his most ambitious construction projects at Kidderminster Ring Road (1973), with the artist using reusable glass-fibre and bespoke polystyrene mould liners to create cast-concrete sections to span a 320m-long (1,050ft) retaining wall. This also included a water feature, seating, and landscaped borders designed with the pedestrian in mind.

One artistic use for his repeat casting process was for the 'Scenes of Contemporary Life' murals (1973) created for a pedestrian subway at in Stevenage New Town. The glass-fibre moulds enabled him to position the imagery in different configurations to provide an unfolding narrative for those wanting to reach the other side of

Subway, Stevenage
Town Centre, UK

a busy dual carriageway. These skills developed within British infrastructure projects gave him the confidence to tackle vast commissions located from ground level, down to concourse and track-side for five stations of the Bay Area Rapid Transit system in San Francisco (1971–5).

And finally, any other examples of Carchitecture around the world you like — service stations, garages, engineering infrastructure, car parks, buildings from that car-mad era of the 50s, 60s and 70s?

In Croydon the labyrinth of subways under the flyover and within the town centre created a concrete and mosaic world during my childhood years, the dark, enclosed spaces suddenly opening up to an overload of senses, with fragmented views of V-shaped pilotis and deck slabs, accompanied by deafening traffic noise. The subways provided a portal, with a feeling of trepidation as you entered and complete disorientation as you exited in an entirely different location.

In the midst of Croydon's post-war building boom emerged an idea to create an inner ring for the town centre, but only three sides surrounding the high-rise area known as 'mini Manhattan' were fulfilled. This resulted in a series of road inventions including a flyover, underpass, dual carriageways, slip roads and subways which would have a huge

impact on those who lived, worked and socialized in Croydon for generations to come.

The first phase, led by borough engineer Allan Holt (1954–66), was to greatly widen Wellesley Road and Park Lane, transforming this semi-residential neighbourhood into a spacious six-lane highway flanked by tall office blocks, with two subways installed to enable pedestrians to cross in safety to the corporation car park and proposed shopping and office developments. The jewel in the crown was a green faience-tiled 335m-long (1,100ft) underpass, descending 7 metres (23ft) beneath an 18m-diameter (60ft) roundabout.

The second and third stages, led by borough engineer H. Marcus Collins with consulting architect D.H. Beaty-Pownall, included the 800m-long (½-mile) 'Croydon flyover', planned to relieve heavy peak-period traffic congestion and provide convenient car parks without traversing pedestrian-clustered streets. By 1967, it began to emerge above the town centre, the *Croydon Advertiser* reporting on the swath of clearance cutting through the old town. Yet, even by 1968, subways were a topic of discussion in the *Design* journal article, 'All hope abandon, ye who enter here?' Regular contributor Hilary Haywood described how these 'human drains' seemed to be the accepted solution in high-density urban areas but wondered why they needed to be so 'lavatorial drab' and 'near-cynically uninformative'.

By late 2019, with Croydon Council increasing the amount of surface-level road crossings near to the central subway locations, it was wondered what to do with the remaining 'obsolete modes of movement'. A competition entitled 'Reimagining Croydon's Subways' was set up to give professionals, locals and students the opportunity to repurpose six subway locations with the intention of bringing some proposals to life.

The winner – 'Croydon Lives' – and most ambitious idea was reserved for the iconic NLA Tower (now No.1 Croydon) site, originally designed by architects Richard Seifert & Partners and engineers Ove Arup & Partners (1968–70). The building had been commissioned by the pension company Noble Lowndes Annuities to provide 'a 23-storey prestige block of distinctive appearance, together with maximum possible car parking storage below ground'. The resulting spiral carpark was achieved by inscribing within the triangle site a 55m (180ft) circle formed by a 50cm-thick (20in) concrete diaphragm wall, and the landscaping included inbuilt planting, a water feature and sunken pedestrian plaza.

The 'Croydon Lives' proposal wanted to 'reappropriate the spaces' for local businesses and the community, focusing on the site's carpark entrance and one remaining subway, made distinctive by its hexagonal paving and tactile corduroy concrete walls, further emboldened by NLA concrete cut-outs inlaid with blue mosaic. The subterranean open-air space and underground subway would evolve into a street-art gallery, 'Croydon Creates', which could act as an epicentre for the local art scene, alongside 'Croydon Eats', a perfect pop-up opportunity for young chefs, local food companies and caterers looking to establish their reputations. This would create something new that could celebrate and embrace the 'grit and authenticity of the 1960's subway architecture' and bring this location back to life.

Sam Burnett

ON SERVICE STATIONS AND AN ECO FUTURE

TOPGEAR MAGAZINE, UK

Sam, what are your favourite service stations? Architecturally, and otherwise. In the UK and then abroad.

My favourite service station to stop at is Beaconsfield — not because it's any good, it's objectively fairly awful (they put a Wetherspoon's in there, for goodness' sake), but because it has it all. Burgers, chicken, Asian noodles, an egg-and-cress sandwich, or perhaps something with edamame beans in it. Tebay services often wins awards for its farm shop and fancy food, but it's too good for my liking. We don't deserve a handmade soft-boiled scotch egg and a view on British motorways. The best services are brutalist and crumbling, with toilets that haven't seen a whiff of spray cleaner in 18 years — you need to go down the M1 for those. They still have that purity of vision, the weirdly naive optimism of the early motorway.

At the other end of the spectrum there's the Aire de la Baie de Somme on the A16 in France, that does have a delightful view and a nice little walk. It doesn't have any grand pretensions, but then you consider that most other French roadside stops are 120 metres (nearly 400ft) of grass, a single picnic bench and a bucket in a hut for you to wee in.

Which other roadside buildings, civil engineering or carchitecture do you like around the world?

I grew in up Coventry; the whole city used to be a delightful advertisement for carchitecture. The ring road (which I once spent 14 hours driving round in an EV for *TopGear*) is a rollercoaster, and the indoor market in the city centre was part of this vision where cars would drive around the rooftops (looking for parking spaces, mostly) while the precincts below were pedestrianized. It was a bonkers idea and people mostly never took to it. The Americans nailed it all back in the 50s, though — the blend of Space Race and lure of the open road created a whole generation of alluringly wacky roadside buildings. Think Route 66, Vegas and drive-in diners.

You are a France expert — which roads or Alphaville-esque architecture do you like there?

There's a lot around a country's national identity that can be discovered in its motorways: the Brits are entirely passive-aggressive road users — no matter how many lanes you add there will still be someone hogging the outside lane on an empty road. It always amazes me how even the French can make do with two lanes on a fast road. The Périphérique works — reliably congested but moving. Can't say that about any road in London.

Previous page and right: Aire de la Baie de Somme, France

The Viaduc de Millau is like a work of art, but then so is the Mont Blanc Tunnel. It's amazing the ingenuity and engineering magic that can be summoned by humankind when it comes to shaving an hour off a motorway trip. The French are never knowingly drab, though. I love that even the toll booths on the autoroutes are always dramatically styled; it does take the edge off having to pay 25 euros to belt down some tarmac in the middle of nowhere.

Can we find ways to move people more efficiently and design cities for everyone and keep people and the Earth happy? Yes, you are prime minister for a day!

I wouldn't want to legislate against the car without creating a public transport environment that means it just doesn't make sense to drive around town. People just want to get somewhere in the quickest and most convenient way possible, and at the moment that means driving yourself. Trams are brilliant to get people around, and I've loved scooter and bike-sharing services in cities around Europe.

If we're going crazy, then I'm getting rid of the roads in some streets entirely and creating community car parks, making public transport free. Rollerblading can replace maths on the national curriculum and only people who don't own a car will be allowed to buy ice cream. All impossible, of course — people say that an Englishman's home is his castle, but I'd argue the same about his car. You'll never get Brits to share cars, we need somewhere to keep our mint imperials. But we definitely need legislators who aren't afraid to upset the nebulous idea of the 'motorist'. People are only motorists until something better comes along. I'd still like to be able to go for a nice drive in the countryside, though, if it's still there.

The Mont Blanc
Tunnel, France / Italy

Rolando Pujol

ON THE TRAIL OF AMERICA'S DINERS, DRIVE-INS AND ROADSIDE DIVES

ROLANDO IS WITH ABC TV IN NEW YORK AND CREATOR OF THERETROLOGIST.COM

Tell us a little about your RETROLOGIST project.

The Retrologist has its roots deep in my marrow — it reflects interests I've cultivated going back to my earliest memories. I've always been intrigued by the built environment and what it says about its times and culture. A hamburger stand that was built in 1950 is different than one built in 1980, and today's is quite different than the previous two. Why? How? Which versions are better? Which stir the soul? Which depresses it? I love digging into these kinds of questions and, even more, finding examples of such on the road.

I'm especially fascinated by commercial architecture and signage built between, say, the 1940s and the 1980s, as well as the evolution of chain businesses of all kinds. The Retrologist approaches this world as though examining a palimpsest, happily peeling back, studying and celebrating those layers, and the stories that go into them.

I first began to write pieces that might be considered Retrologist material in 2005, published in *amNewYork*, where my Endangered NYC advocacy series won a key award and helped get our new tabloid paper noticed. My journey towards the Retrologist as we know it began with a popular blog at *amNewYork* called Urbanite, and my own tweets starting in 2010 — back when Twitter was still Twitter and so much fun. By 2012, I was on Tumblr, where I launched the Retrologist brand and a recognizable version of what you see

Hildebrandt's, USA

today. It wasn't until 2019 that the wider world —
or the world according to Instagram — really took
notice of the Retrologist. I'd been on Instagram
for years, plugging along, but in late 2018, for
a variety of reasons, I felt compelled to embrace
Instagram full-bore as a creative outlet and was
thrilled to see the community I could build there.
My growth there was explosive, which led to
notable profiles of my work, a growing Substack
newsletter, and now a book deal. I couldn't be
more excited about the Retrologist and where it's
taking me and all those I'm lucky to have following
my adventures.

**What are some examples of great roadside
architecture around America you like? The
quirkier the better.**

You know, I'm pretty lower-case catholic in my
tastes. So much fascinates me. I'm curious about
everything. I'll break it down into a few buckets.
One would be quirky roadside curiosities.

Places like the Big Duck in Flanders, New
York, or the Coffee Pot in Bedford, Pennsylvania,
or the 10.5m-tall (35ft) Winnie the Witch in
St James, New York, or the massive 76-brand
gasoline storage tank in Wilmington, California,
that every October is painted as a jack-o-lantern,
called Smilin' Jack. 'Muffler Men' in all kinds of
disguises. The list goes on and on.

McDonald's, USA

Big, attention-grabbing roadside attractions that reflect the ambition and the quirkiness of their creators and times, that entertain, that give back, that make a few bucks. This is such an American conceit – bigger and bolder is better. Let me impress you! Stop here, not there! I also have a thing for the beautiful storefront, achingly precious and pure. To me, few human-created things are more stunning than the storefront of Hildebrandt's Luncheonette, in Williston Park, New York, which was recently saved by two men who poured their hearts, souls and bank accounts into keeping this place from being destroyed.

I'll add the humble ice-cream stand to the list of places I adore. Show me an old Dairy Queen, untouched by so-called progress, and I'll show you what brings me unadulterated joy. I know of so many mom-and-pop ice-cream stands across the country, and their beauty almost brings me to tears. It speaks to an innocence, a simplicity, and a nostalgia for a lost time of youth, of summers of yore, of life full of endless promise and limitless time to realize it, a sense that you can never quite reclaim but always seek as an adult. And when you see young people gathered outside these shops today, on a warm summer night under the yellow fluorescence of an A-frame ice-cream shack, you see them building their own memories that will enrich their lives one day, too.

Dairy Queen, USA

You focus on fast food, too — which are some of the quirkier favourites you have? We talked a lot about your favourite and mine on my podcast Park Date — the Pizza Hut Classic!

Yes! I love playing roadside archaeologist, looking for traces of every iteration of the development of iconic fast-food chains. Take McDonald's, where the hunt for remaining mansard-roofed buildings has become a weekend obsession.

Take Pizza Hut, whose retro Pizza Hut Classics restaurants are the best thing happening in American restaurant design today, as seen through the nostalgic gaze of the Retrologist. I'm so intrigued by these that I put together the most comprehensive list of Pizza Hut Classics out there, and that one Substack post is easily the most popular thing I've ever written.

That says something about how the Retrologist resonates. We are all on journeys to find our own 'Rosebuds', cherished tokens of our past. For many, heaven is a place on Earth, and it's located

Dairy Queen sign, USA

in the dining room of a 1980s-style Pizza Hut.

I also love exploring obscure chains, ones that are down to just a few, places like Rax. Mister Donut is a huge phenomenon in Asia, but in America, there is only one left, in Godfrey, Illinois, and I am embarrassed to admit I've never been to it. My heart will skip a beat when the day comes I see it off in the distance, and burst into the store, trying to conceal my enthusiasm or, if the owner is receptive, unleash it!

What are some of the threats to this Mad Men age of architecture?

Beauty is in the eye of the beholder. And when the beholder's primary motivation is profit, historic architecture, no matter how wondrous or popular on Instagram, will fall.

Fast-food chains have largely gotten architecture wrong over the past decade, replacing cherished, colourful buildings with sleek, grey boxes. I don't think chains need to stay frozen in time, but they can iterate on their heritage in ways that delight, amuse and still keep the brand fresh.

Some brands get it — as I mentioned, Pizza Hut is at the top of the list. Burger King recently brought back a version of their 1969 logo, and it's a fun sighting along the road.

Sky-high rents and the lack of local ordinances to protect historic mom-and-pop shops are my greatest concerns. Look at how we almost lost Hildebrandt's. For every shop that gets saved, countless others do not.

America has a lot on its plate right now, but I do wish we cared more about our Main Street and highway heritage — there is an American instinct to tear down and rebuild, rinse and repeat. I think we can learn a thing or two from Europe, where you have restaurants that have been around for many centuries. Exploring European cities is so compelling because of that palimpsest, those layers. We feel especially connected to our shared humanity through the ages. We need to make sure we save more of our historic shops, storefronts and streetscapes here in the United States.

I'd like to think the Retrologist plays a meaningful role in helping more people understand this. Nothing makes me happier than when somebody tells me they appreciate roadside Americana now, that they see the world around them differently because of my work. I only wish I could do the same in the boardrooms at, say, McDonald's!

Stuart Baird

ON SCOTLAND'S UNIQUE MOTORWAY SYSTEM

CREATOR OF SCOTTISHROADSARCHIVE.ORG.UK

How did you get into roads, cars and engineering?

With there being so many interesting motorway features around Glasgow it would be hard not to have some interest. Driving along the urban M8 as a child really stuck with me, particularly the wonder of large structures such as Kingston Bridge or the Clyde Tunnel. They were all truly fascinating. That fascination with infrastructure generally led me to a career in civil engineering.

Which roadside buildings, civil engineering or Carchitecture do you like around the world?

There are so many to mention! I was particularly impressed by the urban freeways in the USA, especially around Las Vegas. They are so functional and you can get from A to B without having to stop at a junction in many cases. Well, at least when there's no congestion! I also have a love for the German autobahns – long straights, higher speed limits and, occasionally, hedgerows in the central reservation. In the UK my favourite is the Preston bus station with its car park on top. A true post-war legend!

Tunnel over the Clyde expressway, Scotland

Can we find ways to move people more efficiently and design cities for everyone and keep people and the Earth happy in future? Do you see, for example, any radical moves in Glasgow to downgrade or bury motorways like in Birmingham and Boston? To build more cycle lanes or things like that too?

I think we have definitely reached a stage where we need to reconsider how people move around. Public transport plays a key role in that and, just as in the 60s, there is a desire to make it work for more people than it does. Active travel is also key, but I think it needs to be provided where it will have immediate positive impacts and with the support of those living around it. There will always be a need for roads that are separated from pedestrians, for people who need to move about the conurbation quickly for work (or for leisure), and of course for the efficient movement of goods. I wouldn't be surprised if there's some work done to minimize the impact of the M8 on its surroundings — that seems very sensible — but I think a complete downgrade or its removal will be very difficult to achieve in the foreseeable future without causing considerable disruption on other parts of our already constrained roads network!

You are an expert on Scotland — which buildings from this era do you like? And what do you think about the landscapes we created like Cumbernauld, East Kilbride, the urbanism of Glasgow the M8 wrapped around? Scotland has a lot of this for a small country.

Scotland does have a lot of this, unusually, as you say, because we are a small country. It's all very indicative of the genuine optimism of the post-war era, that things could be better and that real investment in infrastructure was a way to achieve it. Our New Towns are fabulous and all unique in their own way, from Cumbernauld's free-flow roads system, East Kilbride's shopping centre and swimming pool and Irvine's impressive bypasses. They were visions of a future that sadly failed to materialize. I'm very much a fan of modernist or brutalist architecture. I'm a real fan of the Charing Cross Tower and the Elmbank Complex around it in Glasgow.

Cumbernauld, Scotland

FURTHER READING & WATCHING

Books:
Concrete Island, J.G. Ballard
Bridge, Lucy Blakstad
Concretopia, John Grindrod
The New Ruins of Great Britain, Owen Hatherley
'City Limits': Infrastructure, Inequality, and the Future of America's Highways, Megan Kimble
Meet Me By The Fountain, Alexandra Lange
Buildings and Infrastructure for the Motor Car (Historic England), John Minnis and Kathryn A. Morrison and edited by Paul Stamper
SOS Brutalism, Various

Films:
Just a Few Debts France Owes to America – Jonathan Meades (BBC)
Take Me High
Telly Savalas Looks At Birmingham
The Secret Life of the Motorway (BBC)

Other:
Retrologist.com
Sabre-roads.org.uk
Scottishroadsarchive.org

Interchange, Las
Vegas, USA

ACKNOWLEDGEMENTS

'Ring Road Poets of Coventry' and 'Leeds — Motorway City of the 70s' were first published in the *Guardian*.

'The DeLorean Story', 'Tunnel Renaissance', 'The Car Park is Being Reinvented', 'Super-sized Sculptures by the Roadside', 'Tees Transporter', and elements of 'Paradise Circus' were all first published in the *Independent*. All are © Independent News & Media.

'Road Racing in Birmingham' was first published in the Emirates magazine — *Open Skies*.

THANKS

Thanks to Sophie Hanbury, Mary Andrews and all at the *Independent*, all at the *Guardian*, Chris Marshall, Lisa Brown, David Ellis, Jack Simpson, Dawn Pereira, Felix Torkar, Sam Burnett, Steve Pill, James Drury, Catherine Croft, Elain Harwood, and the 20th Century Society.

My amazing team at Batsford on the ball as always: Rebecca Armstrong, Nicola Newman, Polly Powell, Frida Green.

Peripherique, Paris, France

INDEX

PICTURE CREDITS

BATSFORD

Publishing Manager **Nicola Newman**
Editor **Rebecca Armstrong**
Art Director **Eoghan O'Brien**
Junior Designer **Sanya Jain**
Layout design by **Kei Ishimaru**
Head of Production **Morna McPherson**
Production Controller **Pete Rouse**

First published in the United Kingdom
in 2025 by
Batsford
43 Great Ormond Street
London
WC1N 3HZ

An imprint of B. T. Batsford Holdings Limited

ISBN 9781849949088

A CIP catalogue record for this book is available from the British
Library.

10 9 8 7 6 5 4 3 2 1

Reproduction by Rival Colour Ltd, UK
Printed by Toppan Leefung Printing International Ltd, China

This book can be ordered direct from the publisher at www.
batsfordbooks.com, or try your local bookshop.

FSC
www.fsc.org
MIX
Paper | Supporting
responsible forestry
FSC® C104723